Charles William Bardeen

Handbook for School Trustees of the State of New York

Giving in convenient form an epitom [!] of the Consolidated school law, of

1894.

Charles William Bardeen

Handbook for School Trustees of the State of New York
Giving in convenient form an epitom [!] of the Consolidated school law, of 1894.

ISBN/EAN: 9783337373597

Printed in Europe, USA, Canada, Australia, Japan

Cover: Foto ©Paul-Georg Meister /pixelio.de

HANDBOOK

FOR

SCHOOL TRUSTEES

OF THE

STATE OF NEW YORK

GIVING IN CONVENIENT FORM AN EPITOM OF THE

CONSOLIDATED SCHOOL LAW OF 1894

WITH REFERENCES TO THE

CODE OF PUBLIC INSTRUCTION

BY

C. W. BARDEEN

EDITOR OF THE SCHOOL BULLETIN

SYRACUSE, N. Y.
C. W. BARDEEN, PUBLISHER
1894

PREFACE

The Consolidated School Law which went into effect on July 1, 1894, makes so many important changes that it must as soon as possible be made thoroughly familiar by every teacher and school officer. But it makes a pamphlet of 135 pages, and it expresses everything with the verbose exactness of legal phraseology, so that it is not always easy at first reading to see just what is meant, and it is often difficult to find just what is wanted.

So this Handbook has been prepared, which arranges the law by subjects, putting what is most important in large print and giving the minor details in notes, so that the gist of the law may be seen at a glance, and then the minor matters looked up as needed. Reference is given for every statement to the law itself, and *references are given to the new Code of Public Instruction*, which has been placed in every district in the State, but which except through the references in this Handbook cannot be used in connection with this law.

The differences between district and union schools are pointed out in detail, and all needed directions are given for establishing an academic department under the Regents of the University, with the law pertaining to the Regents' schools. The Tabular Analysis will be found helpful for class use, and the Index is unusually comprehensive. In short I have spared no pains to make this a complete and convenient manual of New York school law, accurate and thoroughly up to date.

C. W. Bardeen.

Syracuse, Aug. 25, 1894.

CONTENTS

REFERENCES

References to the Consolidated School Law of 1894 are indicated by small figures in parenthesis, the Roman number giving the title, the first arabic number the section, and the second arabic number the subsection. Thus (i. 2) indicates 1st title, 2d section; (xi. 1–7) indicates 11th title, first seven sections; (ii. 13. 5; xiii. 1) indicates 2d title, 13th section, subsection 5, and 13th title, section 1.

When an arabic number is separated from the preceding by a comma instead of a period, it indicates an additional section or subsection. Thus, (vii. 13, 15) indicates 7th title, 13th *and* 15th sections; (vii. 14. 4, 5) indicates 7th title, 14th section, subsections 4 *and* 5.

Some of the titles are in the law subdivided into articles, but these are not distinguished in the references, since they do not interfere with the paragraphing.

References to the Code of Public Instruction, last edition (1887), are indicated by *italic* numbers. Thus (xiv. 1; *492–504, 557*) means 14th title, 1st section; *and* pages 492–504 and 557 of the Code of 1887.

This Code is a volume of 1075 pages, bound in full leather, and giving the explanations and decisions of the State Department. It is still the authority upon all points except where the law has been changed, and by means of this Handbook is made readily available. Copies may be had of the publisher of this volume at $2.50 each.

Copies of the Consolidated School Law may be had free by addressing the Department of Public Instruction, Albany, N. Y.

HANDBOOK FOR SCHOOL TRUSTEES

SUPERINTENDENT OF PUBLIC INSTRUCTION

Election.—Is elected by joint ballot of the Legislature; his term of office is for three years, commencing on the 7th of April next after an election thereto, with a salary of $5,000 a year (i. 2).

He is *ex officio* a regent of the university, and a trustee of Cornell University and of the New York State Asylum for Idiots (i. 6). He has entire charge of teachers' institutes, for the maintenance of which $30,000 a year is appropriated (x. 1–8); and of training classes, for which $60,000 a year is appropriated (xi. 1–7; *657*).

Appeals.—In case of an appeal to him from any act or decision pertaining to common schools, his decision shall be final, and not subject to review in any court (xiv. 1; *492–504, 557*).

THE STATE SCHOOL MONEYS

How made up.—(*a*) The State tax authorized each year by the legislature (ii. 1); (*b*) such portion of the U. S. deposit fund as shall be appropriated; and (*c*) the income of the common school fund, constitute the State school moneys (ii. 4).

How apportioned by the superintendent.—On or before the 20th day of January in each year the superintendent shall set apart:

(1) The amounts required for salaries of (*a*) commissioners; and (*b*) superintendents (see page —);

(2) Such sums as may be appropriated by the legislature for library moneys;

(3) A contingent fund of $6,000;

(4) A sum for the Indian schools equivalent to their proportion upon the basis of distribution (ii. 5);

(5) The sum of $100 to each district for every qualified teacher who has been employed 160 days (ii. 6).

NOTE 1.—Where there has been change of teachers, a succession of qualified teachers entitles the school to its distributive quota (ii. 6).

NOTE 2.—Pupils employed to teach, as monitors or otherwise, do not entitle to teachers' quota (ii. 6).

NOTE 3.—The 160 days include legal holidays but exclude Saturdays. No school shall be in session on a legal holiday (ii. 6). The legal holidays in New York are Jan. 1; Feb. 22; May 30; July 4; the first Monday in Sept.; Dec. 25; each general election day, and each day appointed by the President or by the Governor for thanksgiving, fasting and prayer, or other religious observance. When a holiday falls on Sunday, the following day is a holiday (*Chap. 677, laws of 1892*).

NOTE 4.—The superintendent shall excuse a deficiency not exceeding 3 weeks in any school year caused by a teacher's attendance upon an institute within the county (ii. 6).

He shall then apportion the remainder of the school moneys, and the library moneys separately among the counties of the State according to population, excluding Indians.

NOTE.—In counties containing cities having school acts, the part to which a city is entitled is apportioned to it separately.

How apportioned by commissioners.—On the 3d

Tuesday of March, the commissioners of each county shall meet at the county seat, and apportion the school moneys as follows:

They shall (*a*) set apart and apportion the library moneys; (*b*) credit to each district the amount apportioned by the superintendent; (*c*) add to the remainder any unexpended school moneys in the hands of the supervisors (vii. 54); (*d*) apportion the amount among the districts in proportion to the aggregate days of attendance; (*e*) send to the county treasurer and superintendent duplicate certificates showing the amounts apportioned to each school district; and (*f*) certify to the supervisor of each town the amount of school moneys apportioned to each district (ii. 13).

NOTE.—*Library moneys.*—They shall apportion the library money thus: To each district an amount equal to that which shall have been raised in said district for library purposes, by tax or otherwise; and if the aggregate amount so raised in the districts within the county shall exceed the sum apportioned to the county, the apportionment shall be *pro rata* to the total amount apportioned (ii. 13. 5; xiii. 1-8).

How distributed by the State and county treasurers.—The moneys so apportioned are payable on the 1st day of April succeeding to the county treasurers (ii. 12), who shall, immediately on receiving the commissioners' certificate of apportionment (ii. 16), pay to each supervisor the moneys apportioned to his town, as soon as the supervisor shall have filed a bond approved by the treasurer (ii. 17).

NOTE.—The refusal of the supervisor to give such security is a misdemeanor. In such case the moneys for the town are paid to some other person designated by the county judge (ii. 18).

How distributed by the supervisor.—The supervisor will pay out library moneys only upon the written orders of trustees; and school moneys for teachers' wages only upon written orders of trustees: except that when a collector in any district shall have given bonds, or treasurer shall be elected as required by law, he shall pay over such school moneys to such collector or treasurer (iii. 4; vii. 14. 4, 5; *594–596*, *659*).

NOTE 1.—Where there is more than one trustee in a district, the written order must be signed by a majority of them (iii. 4).

NOTE 2.—In case of a union free school district the moneys both for teachers' wages and for library moneys shall be paid over to the treasurer (iii. 4. 3).

SUPERVISOR

Town school treasurer.—He is the custodian of the school moneys of the town (ii. 16); must give a bond (ii. 17); must report to the superintendent whether there be gospel or school lots and how they are rented (ii. 22); whether the town has a common school fund, and if so how it is applied (ii. 23); sue for and recover penalties (iii. 4. 9; vii. 13, 15); and act when required in the erection or alteration of a school district (vi. 4; *535*), in which case he shall be paid $1.50 a day for his services (vi. 5). If when elected he is a trustee or a member of a board of education he vacates that office (vii. 22; viii. 5).

NOTE 1.—When a district is dissolved he shall sell its property at auction, apply the proceeds to the payment of its debts, and apportion the residue among the owners of taxable property in proportion to their last assessments (vi. 10; *592*, *593*, *647*). He may also sue for any money of the district outstanding (vi. 11).

NOTE 2.—The board of supervisors may divide a school commissioner district which contains more than 200 school districts (*Chap. 686, laws of 1892; 627*).

Report.—On the 1st Tuesday in March he shall make a report in writing to the county treasurer showing the amount of school moneys in his hands, and the districts to which they stand accredited (iii. 3).

NOTE 1.—The supervisor is to keep a true account of all school moneys received and disbursed, and lay the same with proper vouchers before the board of town auditors at each annual meeting thereof (iii. 4. 4). He is also to keep a record of all receipts and disbursements in a bound blank book, which he shall deliver to his successor in office (iii. 4. 5).

NOTE 2.—Within 15 days after the termination of his office, he is to deliver a true account of all receipts and disbursements of school moneys, and deliver the same to the town clerk, etc. (iii. 4. 6; iv. 1. 6-8).

Failure to pay county tax.—Whenever after the first day of March in any year any county has failed to pay its share of the State tax, the State treasurer and superintendent are authorized to make a temporary loan to meet the deficiency, which amount with interest at 12 per cent shall be added to the amount of State tax and levied upon such county by the board of supervisors at the next assessment (ii. 3).

TOWN CLERK

Records.—Shall carefully keep all maps, papers, and records of his office pertaining to common schools (iv. 1; iii. 4, 6; vii. 89).

Reports of trustees.—Is to see that trustees deposit with him at the proper time their annual reports, and to deliver the same to the commissioner; also, to furnish the commissioner the names and post-office addresses of district officers, reported to him by district clerks (iv. 4).

Alteration of boundaries.—Trustees may request the town clerk and the supervisor to be associated with the commissioner in deciding as to change of boundaries of school districts (vi. 4; *535*), in which case he shall be paid $1.50 a day for his services (vi. 5).

SCHOOL COMMISSIONER

Election.—The term of office begins on the 1st of January succeeding the election, and is for 3 years (v. 4).

NOTE.—The years of election are 1896, 1899, etc., except in the second district of Tompkins county, where they are 1895, 1898, etc.

Qualifications.—The candidate must be (*a*) of full age, (*b*) a citizen of the United States, (*c*) a resident of the State and (*d*) of the county in which the district is situated. A trustee or member of a board of education vacates that office when elected commissioner (vii. 22; viii. 5); and a commissioner must not engage in teaching during his term of office (*627*). No person is deemed ineligible on account of sex (v. 3).

Salary.—An annual salary of $1,000 is paid him from the State school moneys. This may be increased by action of the board of supervisors. An allowance of $200 a year is also made by the county for expenses (v. 7–9).

Removal.—If he persistently neglects to perform his duties his salary may be forfeited (v. 10): and he may be removed by the superintendent for wilful violation of duty, or for wilfully disobeying any decision, order, or regulation of the superintendent (i. 13). If he is engaged directly or indirectly as publisher or seller of school books, or in making or selling school apparatus; or if he receives any gift or reward or promise for his influence in securing the sale among schools of books or furniture, he commits a misdemeanor and may be removed from office (v. 12).

Apportionment.—The commissioners of each county shall meet at the county seat on the 3d Tuesday of March in every year, to apportion the school moneys of county among the different districts (ii. 12). See pages 10, 11.

Visitation.—Shall visit schools in his district as often as practicable each year, and make inquiries of all matters relating to the schools, and their management, and the condition of the school property; and recommend to trustees and teachers the proper course of instruction, management, discipline, and studies for the school (v. 13. 2).

Condemnation of schoolhouses.—If he deems a schoolhouse wholly unfit for use he may condemn it, under written order taking effect immediately (vi. 13.4; *629, 630, 636, 637*).

NOTE.—He has also the power to direct the trustees (*a*) to make any repairs or alterations on the schoolhouse or out-buildings which shall, in his opinion, be necessary for the health or comfort of the pupils at an expense not to exceed $200, unless more shall be voted by the district (*637*); (*b*) to repair or replace the school-furniture at an expense not to exceed $100 in any one year. (*c*) He may also direct the abatement of any nuisance on the premises when the cost is not more than $25 (v. 13.3). He is to approve of plans for school-buildings (vii. 17; *639*), and of change of site (vii. 19). He has no power to condemn a schoolhouse *site* (*655*).

Examination of teachers.—Is to examine persons proposing to teach common schools in his district, who do not possess a State certificate or a normal school diploma, and to grant licenses to those found to be qualified (v. 13. 5).

NOTE.—He may have the use of any school-building in his district for holding examinations (v. 16).

Annulment of licenses.—He is to examine any charge affecting the moral character of any teacher within his district, and if he finds the charges sustained to annul the teacher's license (v. 13. 6).

NOTE.—He also has the power to take affidavits, administer oaths, and issue subpœnas, when directed by the superintendent to take testimony in cases of appeal (v. 14).

Teachers' classes.—Teachers' classes, organized in any academy or union school by appointment of the superintendent, are subject to the visitation of the commissioner; it is his duty to advise and assist the principal of such school in the organization and management, and at the close of the term to examine the students in such classes and to issue teachers' certificates to such as show proper qualifications (xi. 7).

Teachers' institutes.—He is to make all necessary

arrangements for institutes when appointed by the superintendent, and report the same (x. 2).

NOTE 1.—He has the right to use any school-building in the district for that purpose (x. 3).

NOTE 2.—All schools in the district must be closed during the institute; except that union free school districts having a population of more than 5,000 and employing a superintendent may be closed or not at the option of the board of education (x. 4). The schools thus closed shall be allowed the same average pupil attendance for the week of the institute as for the week preceding, and any school failing to close shall receive no public money based upon the aggregate attendance during institute week (x. 5). Wilful failure to close the school during institute week is sufficient cause for withholding the public moneys (x. 6).

NOTE 3.—All teachers employed or under contract to teach in the district shall attend the institute and shall receive wages for the time in attendance (x. 4).

District boundaries.—Shall ascertain from time to time if the boundaries of school districts are definitely described in the records of the proper town clerks; in case they are found defective, or are in dispute, shall cause them to be amended, or an amended record to be made (v. 13. 1; vii. 1, 3, 4; *539*).

May alter the boundaries of any district with the written consent of the trustees of the districts affected (vi. 2; vii. 1, 3, 4; *244–257*, *531–534*, *540–563*).

NOTE 1.—If the trustees of any such district refuse to consent, he may make and file with the town clerk his order making the change; but directing that it shall not take effect till a specified day not less than three months after giving notice to the trustees as given below (vi. 3).

Within ten days after filing such order, he shall give to one or more of the assenting and the dissenting trustees of any district affected by the change, at least a week's notice in writing, that, at a named time and place within the town, he will hear the objections to the alteration. The trustees of any such district may request the supervisor and town clerk to be associated with the commissioner; the decision made, whether the order directing the change shall be confirmed or annulled, is final, unless duly appealed from (vi. 4; *534–539*).

NOTE 2.—*Union free school districts.*—He may alter the boundaries of any union free school district whose limits do not correspond with those of a city or an incorporated village in like manner as of common school districts; but no district shall be altered or divided which has any bonded indebtedness outstanding (v. 6; *559*).

NOTE 3.—*Dissolved districts.*—The commissioner shall order the clerk of a dissolved district to deposit the books, papers, and records of the district in the town clerk's office, filing a duplicate of the order with the town clerk (vi. 13). The dissolved district must continue to hold meetings for the sake of paying its just debts (vi. 12). For distribution of its property, see vi. 10; *592*.

NOTE 4.—The inhabitants of a district have no power to annul it (*580*), or to vote that no school be held (*617*).

Reports.—On August 1 he shall make a report to the superintendent, procuring from the town clerk's office the reports of the trustees, and after abstracting the necessary contents, indorse and deposit them with a copy of his abstract in the county clerk's office (v. 16; *200*).

CITY AND VILLAGE SUPERINTENDENTS

Limit of population.—In any incorporated village or union school district having a population of 5,000 or upward, the board of education may appoint a superintendent of schools, to be under their direction, with powers and duties prescribed by them. He shall be paid from the teachers' fund a salary to be fixed by a majority vote. Such superintendent shall entitle the district to receive $800 a year from the free school fund (viii. 17; ii. 5).

NOTE 1.—It is for the State superintendent to determine by causing the enumeration to be made whether the district really has a population of 5,000 (ii. 5; viii. 17).

NOTE 2.—Cities entitled to more than one member of assembly receive an additional $500 for each additional member of assembly (ii. 5).

NOTE 3.—The time of the superintendent must be exclusively devoted to general supervision (ii. 5). He cannot act at the same time as teacher.

ANNUAL AND SPECIAL MEETINGS

Time and place.—The annual meeting shall be held on the first Tuesday in August each year, and unless the hour and place thereof shall have been fixed by a vote of a previous district meeting, the same shall be held in the schoolhouse at 7½ o'clock in the evening (vii. 8; *197, 517, 570–578*).

NOTE 1.—When the time for the annual meeting shall pass without a meeting being held, and the trustees or clerk shall not call a special meeting within 20 days thereafter, the school commissioner or superintendent may order a meeting at which the annual reports shall be made and officers elected (vii. 9, 15; *584*).

NOTE 2.—The proceedings may be set aside if the attendance was too small to make its action fairly represent the wishes of the district (*582*).

Districts of 300 children.—Districts where the number of children of school age exceeds 300, as shown by the last annual report of the trustees, may by a majority vote at any annual meeting determine that the election of officers shall thereafter be held by ballot on the Wednesday next following the first Tuesday in August each year, between 12 o'clock noon and 4 o'clock in the afternoon, at the principal schoolhouse, or at such other suitable place as the trustees may designate on due notice (vii. 15).

NOTE 1.—The annual meeting in such districts shall be held as usual on Tuesday evening, when all business, except the election of officers, shall be transacted (vii. 8).

NOTE 2.—This paragraph does not apply to cities, nor to union free school districts whose boundaries correspond with those of an incorporated village, nor to any district organized under a special act prescribing the manner of the election of officers, nor to the counties of Erie, Richmond, St. Lawrence, Suffolk, Warren, and Westchester (vii. 15).

NOTE 3.—When the place of election is other than the schoolhouse, the trustees shall give notice thereof at least one week before, by posting the same in five conspicuous places in the district, or by publishing it in a local newspaper (vii. 15).

NOTE 4.—The trustees may by resolution extend the time of holding the election from four o'clock till sunset (vii. 15).

Special meetings.—To call a special meeting, a notice shall be duly served upon each inhabitant entitled to vote, at least five days before the meeting; the notice shall state the purposes for which the meeting was called and no other business shall be transacted (vii. 6; *578, 579, 584, 646*).

NOTE.—The notice shall be read in the hearing of each qualified voter or, if he is absent from home, a copy shall be left at least six days before the meeting, stating the time, place, and object of the meeting (vii. 2; *579*).

But unless it shall appear that an omission to give due notice to all such voters was wilful and fraudulent, no proceedings shall be held illegal for want of such notice (vii. 7: *588, 646*).

NOTE.—The proceedings of any meeting may be set aside where the proceedings were so turbulent and disorderly as to prevent a fair expression of opinion (*589*), or where records of the meetings were not properly kept (*591*). But the meeting is not bound by strict parliamentary rules, and makes its own (*573*).

Qualification of voters.—Every person, man or woman, (*a*) of 21 years of age, (*b*) who has resided in the district for the preceeding 30 days, (*c*) a citizen of the United States; and (1) who owns or hires or holds under contract to purchase real property in such district liable to taxation for school purposes (*790*), or (2) who is a parent of a child of school age that has attended the district school at least 8 weeks within one year preceeding; or (3) who has permanently residing with him or her any such child; or (4) who owns and was assessed on the last preceding assessment roll of the town exceeding $50 of personal property, exclusive of such as is exempt from execution, and no other, shall be entitled to vote at any school meeting, and may vote upon all questions brought before the meeting, including propositions to raise money by tax (*638*) (vii. 11).

NOTE 1.—The voter must have *all* the qualifications (*a*), (*b*), (*c*), and *one* of the qualifications (1), (2), (3), (4). An alien is no longer permitted to vote. See *187*, *528*, *788–791*.

NOTE 2.—Under (2) both father and mother are entitled to vote.

NOTE 3.—Under (3) only one person, the head of the household, is entitled to vote. Therefore where husband and wife residing together have such a child residing with them, the wife is not on that account entitled to vote.

NOTE 4.—Under (1) a man does not become eligible through real estate owned by his wife (*791*).

NOTE 5.—No person shall be deemed ineligible to vote at any district meeting or to serve as any school officer, by reason of sex, who has the qualifications required by law (vii. 11; *791*.)

Illegal voting.—Any person offering to vote at school meeting, upon being challenged as unqualified by any legal voter, shall be permitted to vote (*522*) on making this declaration: "I do declare and affirm that I am an actual resident of this school district and that I am qualified to vote at this meeting." If the person refuses to make this declaration, the vote of such person shall be rejected. (vii. 12, 16.)

NOTE. Any person who, upon being so challenged, shall wilfully make a false declaration of his or her right to vote at such election is guilty of a misdemeanor. Any unqualified person who shall vote, though not challenged, shall forfeit the sum of $5.00, if it be at an ordinary district meeting (vii. 13,), or of $10 if it be an election held on the Wednesday following the annual meeting (vii. 15), to be sued for by the supervisor for the benefit of the district (vii. 13, 15). See Penal Code 41 k. 5, 18.

Powers of school meeting.—The inhabitants may by majority of the votes of those present (vii. 4):

(1) Appoint a chairman (*191*).

(2) In the absence of the clerk appoint a clerk *pro tem.*

NOTE.—At the annual meeting, the next business is the presentation of the annual reports of trustees, collector, and treasurer (vii. 35, 86). The trustees then present statement of the money needed for teachers' wages, fuel, repairs, insurance, furniture, library, etc. (vii. 14), and the meeting takes action upon it. This should precede election.—(*Superintendent's Circular of Information*, July 5, 1894; *407*).

(3) Adjourn from time to time as needed (*192, 572, 577, 751*).

(4) Elect by ballot (*a*) trustee or trustees, (*b*) district clerk, (*c*) district collector, and if so determined by the district (*d*) a treasurer (*515–529*).

NOTE 1.—No school commissioner or supervisor may be trustee, and no person can hold two district offices at the same time (*419, 518, 785, 786*). Every district officer must be a resident of the district, qualified to vote at its meetings, and able to read and write (vii. 22, 23). The treasurer must also be a taxable inhabitant (vii. 14. 5). If the candidate receiving a majority is found to be ineligible, a new election must be had (*525*). The trustee must not be the teacher of the district (*744, 765*).

NOTE 2.—The term of office of all district officers is one year, except that where there are three trustees the term is for three years, and in changing from one trustees to three, one trustee is elected for two years. But district officers hold office until their successors are elected or appointed (vii. 24). In a newly-created district the terms of the officers elected expire on the 1st Tuesday of August next thereafter (vii. 25).

NOTE 3.—It requires a *majority* vote to elect; that is the candidate must receive more votes than all the other candidates together (vii. 14. 4; *517, 524*).

NOTE 4.—Formerly election by ballot was required only in union school districts (*517, 521, 526*), but it is now required in all districts (vii. 14. 4).

(5) Determine to have a treasurer.

(6) Fix the amount of bonds of the collector and of the treasurer.

(7) Designate sites for a schoolhouse (*273–287, 581, 641*).

NOTE 1.—The final designation can be made only at a special meeting of the district duly called for the purpose by a written resolution in which the proposed site is described.

NOTE 2.—While the district remains unaltered, the site cannot be changed without written consent of the commissioner and a majority vote of the district (vii. 19; *276, 642–657*). The old site may then be sold (vii. 20).

NOTE 3.—For acquisition of site by condemnation, see ix. 1—5.

(8) To vote a tax for purchasing, leasing, and improving such site (*258–264, 686*).

NOTE 1.—No tax exceeding $500 for a schoolhouse can be levied unless the commissioner shall certify his approval (*489, 568*), nor shall the house be built till the commissioner shall approve in writing the plan of ventilating, heating, and lighting (vii. 17; *639*).

NOTE 2.—By a majority vote, the money for school building may be raised by instalments, not to extend more than 20 years. The trustees may then borrow at not more than 6 per cent., and issue bonds (vii. 18).

NOTE 3.—The district is not limited as to the amount it may pay for a site (*642*).

NOTE 4.—The district must purchase the site. A perpetual lease will not be permitted (*650, 685*).

NOTE 5.—All voting upon questions that involve the expenditure of money or the levying of tax *must be by ballot*, or by taking and recording the ayes and noes (vii. 14. 18).

NOTE 6.—A meeting may within proper time increase, diminish, or rescind the action of a former meeting to build a schoolhouse (*587*).

(9) To vote a tax not exceeding $25 in any one year for the purchase of maps, globes, and school apparatus, and for the purchase of text-books and other school necessaries for the use of poor scholars of the district (*193*).

NOTE 1.—This section does not authorize the adoption of free text-books (*193*).

(10) To vote a tax for a school library.

(11) To vote a tax to supply deficiency from what has proved incollectible of a former tax (*193*).

(12) To authorize the trustees to have the school property insured by any insurance company created by or under the laws of this State. See vii, 47. 7; *266*.

(13) To alter repeal and modify their proceedings as needed (*193*).

(14) To vote a tax for a book to record the proceedings (*194*).

(15) To vote a tax to replace moneys lost or embezzled by district officers, and to pay expenses of law suits (*195*).

(16) To vote a tax for teachers' wages.

(17) To vote a tax to pay judgments against the district (*745–747*, *752*, *754–756*).

NOTE 1.—When the court shall certify that school officers have acted in good faith and where the matter might have been appealed to the superintendent, no costs in actions at law shall be allowed to plaintiff (xv. 3). When school officers have been instructed by the district to bring or defend an action, their costs and reasonable expenses shall be a district charge (xv. 4). When they have brought or defended such action without vote of the district, they may be reimbursed by a majority vote at a district meeting (xv. 5). Should the district refuse, they may appeal to the county judge (xv. 6).

NOTE 2.—In all propositions to spend or raise money, the vote shall be by ballot, or by taking the ayes and noes (vii. 14).

DISTRICT CLERK

Duties.—He is (1) to record district proceedings; (2) give notice of special meetings; (3) post notices of adjourned meetings; (4) give notice of annual meeting; (5) notify persons elected to district offices; (6) notify trustees of resignations; (7) keep all records and transfer them to his successor, or in dissolved districts (8) to the town clerk; (9) attend and record meetings of trustees; (10) call special meetings when the office of trustee is vacant; (11) hold the records open for inspection (vii. 34; *508–511*).

NOTE.—The law does not permit the clerk to receive pay for his services (*510*).

Notices of election.—Shall notify in writing any person elected to any district office of such an election, when the person is not present at the meeting. Unless a written refusal to serve is filed with the clerk within 5 days thereafter, such person shall be deemed to have accepted the office (vii. 27, 34. 5).

Penalties.—If the clerk fails to deliver the records to his successor, or if in a dissolved district he fails on order of the commissioner to deliver them to the town clerk, he forfeits $50 (vii. 13, 34).

DISTRICT COLLECTOR

Bond required.—Vacates his office by not executing a bond, and the trustees may supply the vacancy (vii. 28). If the trustees approve the bond, they shall endorse their approval thereon, and furthermore deliver the bond to the town clerk, who shall file the same in his office, charging the district a fee of 25 cents (vii. 80, 88; *511–514*).

NOTE.—He cannot legally enforce the collection of any tax unless he has executed a bond to the trustees, and renders himself liable for trespass to attempt to collect by levy and sale (Letter, Sup't Rice, Nov. 13, 1865).

It is not sufficient to say that no loss has happened to the district in the past for want of a bond; the inhabitants are entitled to one as security in the future (*511*).

Vacancy.—A refusal to serve as collector creates a vacancy in the office, which the trustees may fill by appointment (Sup't Rice, Letter, April 10, 1854).

NOTE.—A verbal appointment of a collector by the trustee is invalid; the appointment must be written and filed with the district clerk. (Supreme Court—1876.)

Delivery of warrant.—A warrant for the collection of a tax voted by the district shall not be delivered to the collector till the 31st day after the tax was voted; a warrant for any other tax may be delivered when it is completed (vii. 78, 79).

Renewal of warrant.—The collector's warrant may be renewed but once without the written consent of the supervisor to a renewal endorsed thereon (vii. 83; *744*).

Posting notices.—On the receipt of a warrant, the collector shall post notices in at least three public places of the district, one of which shall be on the outside of the front door of the schoolhouse, that he has received such warrant, and that taxes may be voluntarily paid him during the next two weeks. He shall also give notice personally or by mail at least 10 days before the expiration of the two weeks, to the ticket-agent at the nearest railroad station of any railroad assessed, and to non-resident tax-payers where the amount of tax exceeds one dollar (vii. 81).

Compensation.—He shall receive 1 per cent on all sums paid within two weeks of posting the said notice, and 5 per cent on sums thereafter collected.

In case of levy and sale, he shall be entitled to travelling fees at the rate of 10 cents a mile (vii. 81).

Enforcement of tax levy.—At the expiration of a collector's warrant, if the uncollected sums be payable by any person not residing in the district at the time of making out the tax list, or who shall not reside therein at the expiration of such warrant, or if the property assessed be real estate belonging to an incorporated company, and no goods or chattles can be found whereon to levy the tax, the trustees may sue for and recover the same in their name of office (vii. 85).

May sell personal property, but not real estate.—Is under no circumstances authorized to sell real estate; but he can keep levying on personal property till enough to satisfy the tax is secured. (Sup't Rice—Letter April 23, 1866.)

NOTE 1.—No property is exempt from levy and sale under a tax-list and warrant, except certain military equipments. (Code of 1868; p. 191.)

NOTE 2.—The collector may levy upon any goods or chattels lawfully in the possession of the person liable for the tax, although such person be not the owner. (Code of 1868; p. 191. Supreme Court—1835.)

Money held in trust.—He shall keep in his possession all moneys received or collected by him, and pay them out upon orders from the trustees; and he shall report in writing at the annual meeting of all his collections and disbursements, and pay over to his successor, when he gives bail, the moneys belonging to the district. He shall also report to the supervisor on or before the first Tuesday in

March of each year the amount of school moneys in his hands (vii. 86).

He must make good to the district any moneys lost by lack of proper effort to collect (vii. 87).

Unpaid taxes.—If at the expiration of a tax-warrant, any tax of real estate, or taxes upon non-resident stockholders in banks organized under the laws of congress, shall remain unpaid, the collector shall deliver to the trustees an account of the taxes remaining due, with a description of the lands upon the tax-list, with the amount of the tax thereon, and upon making oath before any officer authorized to administer oaths that, after diligent efforts, he has been unable to collect the same, he shall be credited by the trustees with the amount thereof (vii. 72).

NOTE.—The trustees, upon sending the account, affidavit, and their certificate that such account is correct, to the county treasurer, shall be paid the amount of the returned taxes from the county treasury (vii. 73, 74).

TREASURER

An optional office.—Any district may by a majority vote elect a treasurer, as custodian and disbursing officer of all school moneys. He must be a qualified voter and taxable inhabitant of the district (vii. 14.5, 35; iii. 4. 1).

TRUSTEES

Number.—A district having three trustees may at any annual meeting decide by resolution to have but one; no election of a trustee shall be held in such district till the expiration of the terms of those then in office. To change from one trustee to three trustees requires a two-thirds vote of those present at any annual meeting (vii. 26 ; *418*).

Office vacated.—A trustee who publicly declares that he will not accept or serve in the office of trustee, or who neglects to attend three successive meetings of the board (where districts have more than one trustee) after due notice thereof, without a good and valid excuse to the others, vacates the office (vii. 30 ; *766*). A duly qualified person appointed to a school district office who refuses to serve shall forfeit $5 ; or if he does not refuse but neglects to perform his duties he shall forfeit $10, for the benefit of the schools of the district. But if his resignation be offered and accepted by the commissioner or the district meeting there shall be no forfeit (vii. 33).

Removal.—The superintendent may remove a trustee for neglect, or disobedience of orders (*756–762*), but not for immorality (*761*), or for failure to agree with his associates (*760*).

Vacancies.—In case of death, refusal to serve, removal from the district (*787*), or vacancy in the office of trustee by any other cause, and no election of a new trustee by a district meeting within a month thereafter, the commissioner may, in writing, appoint a competent person, to serve until the next annual meeting (vii. 29 ; *192*).

Other vacancies.—Trustees may fill vacancies in other district offices by appointment (vii. 31).

NOTE.—Every appointment to fill a vacancy made by the commisoner or trustees, is to be filed at once with the district clerk, who shall immediately notify the person appointed (vii. 32).

Board meetings.—Any trustee may call a meeting of the board by giving the others at least 24 hours' notice (vii. 45).

NOTE.—When all have been notified and two only meet, these two have the powers of all three (vii. 45). Where there is a vacancy, the two have the powers of all three, and if there are two vacancies, the remaining trustee has the powers of all three (vii. 46). But the acts of a majority are illegal when performed without notifying or consulting all three (Sup't Mŏrgan, Nov. 16, 1848). See *423*, *541*, *543*, *569*, *713–719*, *727*, *743*.

Powers and duties.—The trustees shall:

(1) Call special meetings when needed (vi. 47. 1; *183*).

(2) In the absence of the clerk, give notice of meetings (vii. 47. 2).

(3) Make out a tax list within 30 days after the tax is voted by a district meeting (*328–377*).

NOTE 1.—The law is merely directory; the tax list may be made out after the 30 days (*328*).

NOTE 2.—The tax list shall contain as a heading a statement of the purposes for which the different items of the tax are levied (vii. 47.3, 62).

NOTE 3.—The valuation of taxable property shall be ascertained, so far as possible, from the last assessment roll of the town; where it cannot be so determined, or where any person shall claim a reduction of his assessment, the trustees shall ascertain the true value of the property from the best evidence in their power, giving notice to the persons interested and proceeding the same as required by law of town assessors (vii. 64, 65; *506–508*).

NOTE 4.—Any person working land under contract shall be deemed the possessor, and any person in possession of property under contract to purchase shall be liable to taxation therefor (vii. 67). Every person owning real property who shall improve and occupy the same by his agent or his servant shall be considered a taxable inhabitant of the district (vii. 68). A tenant may charge back to the owner the district tax for schoolhouse property (vii. 69).

NOTE 5.—Lands of non-residents liable to taxation in the district, not occupied by a tenant or improved by the owner, his agent, or servant, are to be assessed as non-resident, and a description thereof entered on the tax-list (vii. 63, 71).

NOTE 6.—In making out a tax list where districts have more than one trustee, *all* of them must be notified in order to meet and act together in determining the assessments: without such notice a tax list is invalid. Sup't Van Dyck—1849; *662*.)

NOTE 7.—When trustees make an original assessment for a school tax, a 20 days' notice to the parties affected is required before the delivery of the tax list and warrant to the collector (*680*).

NOTE 8.—When a person appears before the trustees at the proper time and place to claim a reduction in an original assessment made by the trustees, it is the duty of such trustees to examine the person under oath, and to correct the assessments if they appear to be erroneous (*684*).

NOTE 9.—The tax list may be amended and corrected, with consent of the superintendent (vii. 84).

Limit to tax for building.—No tax exceeding $500, voted by a district meeting for building, hiring, or purchasing a schoolhouse, shall be levied by the trustees without the written approval of such larger sum by the commissioner; and no schoolhouse shall be built in any district until the plan of such schoolhouse, so far as ventilation, heat, and lighting is concerned, shall be approved in writing by the commissioner. But nothing herein contained shall invalidate any tax levied for building and repairing schoolhouses which in other respects comply with existing statutes (vii. 17; *489*).

NOTE 1.—Except in New York city and Brooklyn, all school buildings more than two stories high must have outside stair-cases (vii. 49).

NOTE 2.—A taxable inhabitant who has been within four years set off from another district without his consent, and who has within that period paid into that district a tax for building a schoolhouse shall be exempted from paying tax for building a schoolhouse (vii. 70).

Unfit schoolhouses.—The school commissioner alone has the power to condemn a schoolhouse and school furniture when, in his judgment, it is unfit for use and not worth repairing. When the order reciting the reasons for this action, with a statement of the cost, not to exceed $800, of such new building as is required, has been received by the trustees, they must immediately call a special meeting to consider the question of rebuilding (v. 13. 4; *265*, *629–637*).

NOTE 1.—The meeting shall have no power to reduce the commissioner's estimate of cost more than 25 per cent, and where no tax shall have been voted by the district within 30 days from the time of the first meeting held to consider the question, the trustees shall contract for the building of a schoolhouse to cost not more than the estimate of the commissioner and not to exceed 25 per cent less, and levy a tax to pay for the same (v. 13. 4).

NOTE 2.—A district cannot be compelled to rebuild where the schoolhouse has been destroyed, but the district may be annulled (*559*).

(4) Annex to the tax-list a warrant directed to the collector. See page 26.

NOTE—Within 15 days after the tax-list and warrant are returned by the collector, they must file the same with town clerk (vii. 89).

(5) Purchase or lease a site for the schoolhouse. See page 23.

NOTE.—Trustees are the only legal authority by which the vote of a district can be carried into execution, and have sole power of making contracts and of accepting work done (*632*, *749*).

(6) Have custody of the school property (vii. 47. 6; *266*).

NOTE 1.—They may permit the schoolhouse to be used for instruction in learning, or in music (vii. 52); and must allow it to be used for teachers' institutes or for teachers' examinations, when requested by the commissioner (v. 16.; x. 31). But they must not allow it to be used for temperance meetings (*649*), and should use discretion in opening it for religious meetings; no use should be permitted likely to occasion controversy (*267*).

NOTE 2.—The trustees are especially directed to take care of the code of public instruction, and deliver it to their successors (xv. 12).

(7) Insure the school property (vii. 47. 7; *266*). See also vii. 14.

(8) Insure the school library (vii. 47. 8).

(9) Employ teachers as needed (vii. 47. 9; *744*).

Qualified teachers.—No school moneys or money raised by tax may be paid to a teacher who is not 16 years old, and who does not hold either (*a*) a normal diploma, (*b*) a State certificate, (*c*) a college certificate, (*d*) a uniform certificate, or (*e*) a temporary license (vii. 38; i. 10; *378–394*, *709*, *732*). Any trustee paying public money to an unqualified teacher commits a misdemeanor, and any fine imposed upon him shall be for the benefit of the district (vii. 39, 40).

NOTE.—The teacher's license may be annulled for wilful failure to attend institute (x. 6), for refusal to fulfil a contract (vii. 47. 9), for immorality (v. 13. 6), or for incompetency (*692–698*, *702*). The contract then ceases (*712*). The teacher may be discharged at any time on failure to produce certificate (*732*).

Not limited by the wishes of the district.—Trustees may hire whom they choose for teacher, and pay such wages as they may see fit, with no power by the district or vote of a district meeting to restrain them (*728*); however, the wishes of the inhabitants should not be disregarded (*715*).

A sole trustee has all the powers of a board of three trustees (vii. 44).

NOTE.—Hence he can now employ a teacher for the ensuing year in advance of the school meeting, a power not conferred by the old law.

Relationship.—Trustees shall employ as teacher in a district school no one who is related by blood or marriage to any such trustee, except with the approval of two-thirds of the voters present and voting upon the question at an annual or special meeting. Nor shall the trustees of any district hire a teacher for more than a year in advance. Any person employed in disregard of these provisions shall have no claim for wages against the district, but may enforce the contract made against the trustees consenting to such employment. (vii. 47.9).

NOTE 1.—*Relationship to trustees.*—Where the district has three trustees, a relative of any one of them cannot be hired by the other two unless a meeting of the district approve of it by a two-thirds vote (*721*).

NOTE 2.—The law formerly made the limit of relationship two degrees (*395–399*), but the amended law makes no limit as to relationship and it is to be construed literally. The trustee cannot hire a teacher who is related to him in any degree—(*Letter of Sup't Crooker, Aug. 15, 1894*).

NOTE 3.—The prohibition regarding the employment of a relative as a teacher now applies to union schools, but may be waived upon consent in writing of two-thirds of the members of the board of education (viii. 11).

NOTE 4.—Relationship by marriage ceases upon the death of the wife or husband.

(10) Make with teachers employed a written contract, with stipulation that wages shall be paid monthly (vii. 47. 10; xv. 17, 18; *395, 400, 405, 722.*)

NOTE 1.—A contract with a teacher shall not be made for a shorter time than 10 weeks, or for more than one year in advance (vii. 47.9; *735*).

NOTE 2.—Any failure on part of the teacher to complete an agreement to teach without good reason will be deemed sufficient ground for revoking the certificate (vii. 47.9).

NOTE 3.—The contract may be annulled if the teacher close school upon any school day (*731*).

NOTE 4.—If a teacher gives up his school because the trustees will not sustain him in enforcing reasonable rules, he may recover wages for the time taught (*703*). It is the duty of the trustees if they learn that serious disturbance at school is threatened, to warn the teacher, and to be present themselves (733).

NOTE 5.—Where the teacher gives up the school voluntarily, even at the request of the trustees, she can recover wages only for the time taught (*704*). A teacher giving up the school through sickness is to be paid for the time taught (*723*).

NOTE 6.—When a teacher finds the schoolhouse locked against him, and without applying to the trustee goes away without making demand till 15 days afterward for opportunity to continue, he is held to have abandoned his contract (705).

NOTE 7.—If the school is closed during his term through fear of an epidemic, the teacher is entitled to wages for the time (*710*) ; and if extra weeks are taught, to extra wages for the extra time (*708*). The teacher cannot be compelled to teach an extra week to make up for the institute (*711*), and all holidays are allowed him without loss of wages (*719*).

NOTE 8.—A contract for a year includes the two months of vacation (*707*); but during these months the teacher may teach another school or otherwise employ his time (*710*).

NOTE 9.—When the contract states that it shall continue as long as the teacher keeps a good school, if the teacher is discharged it is for him to prove that he kept a good school (*723*, *726*, *729*).

Dismissal of teachers.—The annulment of the license dissolves all contracts entered into by virtue of its sanction, but until the license is revoked, the trustees are not bound to retain a teacher obnoxious to the district through immorality, ignorance, or inefficiency (*729–734*).

NOTE.—This would be subversive of the principles already enunciated as pertaining to the essential nature of contracts. It cannot be supposed that in case a charge of gross immorality, specifically urged, carrying with it a strong presumption of its truth, were brought against a teacher, the trustees must wait for the tedious delay of a formal hearing before a commissioner, and abide the event which may be determined through insufficiency of evidence, while the moral conviction of the truth of the charges preferred is still strong and abiding. The presence among pupils of a teacher against whom such suspicion should rest, must of itself, from the suggestions to which it would give rise, promote conditions of mind opposed to the development of virtue and purity of the heart.

This consideration alone would justify the trustees in a summary dismissal of the teacher. This, to be sure, is an extreme case, but it is sufficient to illustrate and to establish the principle advanced, that the trustees may be justified in the discharge of a teacher before the close of the term specified in his contract. In determining what constitutes such justification, it is difficult, not to say impossible, to establish uniform rules (*730*).

The power to dismiss the teacher rests with the trustees. For an abuse of their discretion, or an unwarranted exercise of their authority, they are of course responsible. On complaint of the person sustaining what he considers a grievance or wrong, the issue becomes one of fact, and it devolves upon the trustees to show by evidence that the teacher lacked the character, the ability, or the will essential to a proper discharge of his duties, and that he failed thus to fulfil the obviously implied conditions of his contract (*730*).

NOTE.—The mere fact of dissatisfaction on their part, or that of the inhabitants, is not sufficient to justify the discharge of a teacher employed for a definite period. The tribunal before whom the action is brought, as a court, a jury, or the superintendent, are the constituted judges of fact, and will determine, from the evidence presented, whether the incompetence of the teacher, as resulting from ignorance or indifference, is fully proved, and hence his discharge upon the ground of a violated contract clearly justified.

In the case here presented, the trustees offer evidence bearing upon the management and general deportment of the appellant in the school-room, and his intercourse with his pupils, tending to show disregard of the properties and courtesies incident to his position. *Trifling and irrelevant conversation, oft indulged and long continued with pupils in school hours; prying and impertinent questions in regard to domestic affairs; low, and at the least suggestively vulgar, remarks to the older female pupils; rude, boisterous, and harsh language, as a means of or substitute for discipline*, are alleged and proved by the testimony of his pupils, with a circumstantial minuteness that requires emphatic denial or plausible explanation to invalidate or palliate.

The appellant has failed to meet the issue. It is proper and just to remark, that the justification of the trustees does not proceed from any alleged or proved inability or immorality of the appellant; his literary qualifications and his moral character stand unimpeached, and, it is to be hoped, unimpeachable. But his inefficiency appears to have been the result of gross negligence and indifference—a *debilitated will*, rather than of inherent depravity or defective scholarship, a fault which is earnestly hoped the wholesome practical discipline of this experience will serve to eradicate.

Under the view of the case as above presented, therefore, I must decline to interfere with the action of the trustees, and hold that they have presented a sufficient justification therefor (*730*).

The teacher may be dismissed for unjustifiable severity of punishment (732), but not for mere difference of opinion from the trustee as to discipline (732).

(11) Establish school regulations and courses of study (vii. 47. 11).

The principal subject of rules and regulations are the following :

(*a*) ATTENDANCE.—The schools are free to all persons over 5 and under 21 years of age residing in the district (vii. 36).

Children of school age, in the trustee's report, include all children over 5 and under 21 years of age, who on the 30th of June last preceding the date shall have been actually in the district, comprising a part of the family of their parents, guardians, or employers, residing, even but temporarily, in the district; but not including the children of a family residing in another district in which such children may be by law included in the report of its trustees; nor any children supported at a county poor-house or orphan asylum, nor any Indian children on reservations provided with separate schools (vii. 36, 37, 60 ; *207*, *209*, *605*, *608–611*).

NOTE 1.—As a general rule, if the child whose parents or guardians live out of the district is residing, even if temporarily, in the district in good faith and not to avoid the payment of tuition, such child should be enumerated ; otherwise in the district where its parents or guardians reside. It is for the trustee to determine this, after fairly considering the circumstances. Children visiting or boarding are to be enumerated where they permanently reside. (1886—Sup't Morrison.)

NOTE 2.—Non-resident pupils may be admitted into school upon written consent of the trustees upon such terms as the trustees prescribe (vii. 36; *603–605*). When so admitted, the teacher may not refuse to instruct them (*604*).

NOTE 3.—Colored children must be admitted, except when in union free school districts a separate school has been provided (xv. 28, 29; *514*).

NOTE 4.—Fines cannot be imposed upon pupils, and attendance suspended till paid (*601*).

Suspension and expulsion.—Trustees may expel pupils for open, gross immorality manifested by any licentious propensities, language, manners, or habits, though not manifested by acts of licentiousness, or immorality within the school,* or for such violent insubordination against reasonable and proper regulations of the school as to render it impossible to maintain necessary discipline and order, or when in their judgment the good order and proper government of the school demands it (*770*).

Suspension for tardiness.—In 1853, the superintendent decided that "teachers have the right to close the doors of their school-room against all pupils who may claim admission fifteen minutes after the time of opening the school" (Decision No. 1687). Later decisions have ruled that the teacher should not keep tardy pupils in the entry, especially in cold weather (*605*).†

NOTE—In Wisconsin, the superintendent decides that "to lock the door against tardy pupils, say at ten o'clock, is of doubtful propriety. The schoolhouse is a public place. The tardiness may not be the fault of the child. It might be a serious discomfort to the child to be turned back home. Let the school be made attractive." And again: "Tardiness is, of course, a great annoyance. It is difficult to say how far the courts would sustain rules excluding pupils from school for being late. It is doubtful whether it

* 38th Mass. Report, p. 159.

† See also Ill. 356, 553: 87 Ill. 303.

is good policy to turn tardy scholars into the street, perhaps to get into mischief; perhaps to suffer from cold, from waiting outside; certainly to lose more time. Persuasion, attractive lessons in the morning, an attractive school, privation of recesses, final degradation to a lower class if all fails, would perhaps be better remedies."—*Wis. Journal of Ed'n, 1877, p. 125.*

Suspension for absence.—In 1875 the board of education of Hornellsville, N. Y., adopted a rule that in every case of absence of a pupil for more than five days during any term for any other cause than sickness or death in the family, or religious observance, the absentee should be suspended until the beginning of the next term. Its legality being questioned, the superintendent replied:

Under the provisions of the law cited in your letter of the 19th inst., your board of education possesses the power to suspend pupils from school for causes which seem to merit such treatment. In my judgment, however, it would be unwise to enforce strictly the rule referred to in your letter. The object and intention of the law is to get pupils into the schools—not to keep them out.

In another case the same superintendent, Mr. Gilmour, went still further.

Among the regulations of District No. 2, Ellington, was this:

Any scholar absenting himself from any examination or part thereof, appointed by the teachers, without necessity duly certified beforehand, either by himself or his parent or guardian, shall not be admitted to the school afterwards, except by permission of the board and the approval of the principal.

On Feb. 4, 1875, before the written examination, the mother of three boys asked by written note that they be excused from the last days of the term, and withdrew them from the school. On the opening of the next term, the three boys were refused admission under the above rule, the note not being accepted as a sufficient compliance with the regulation. This was over-ruled by Sup't Gilmour, who decided that boards of education have no right to make any regulation under which children are liable to perpetual exclusion from school for an act of the parent (*603*).

This view was carried still further under Sup't Ruggles. In September, 1884, the St. Johnsville board of education established the following rules:

> The principal and teachers of the different rooms may suspend pupils under their immediate control for: 1. Three cases of absence, unless the absence be caused by personal sickness, or serious illness or death in the family, or by some pressing emergency. But one case of absence can be counted in the same day. * * *
>
> The power of reinstatement shall be limited to the board of education or the principal. * * *
>
> Any pupil suspended for any cause shall not be entitled to any privileges of the school until reinstated.

For four such absences the father of Clarence Sanders refused to give any reason; and on Nov. 5, the boy was suspended, and on presenting himself at school the next day was refused admission. His father appealed to the State department, which on March 20, 1885, decided that the boy must be reinstated, on the grounds (1) that the power of suspension should not be delegated from the board to a teacher; (2) that to require the parent to state the particular cause for a child's absence or detention is not only unnecessarily inquisitorial, but, logically carried out, would permit the teacher or trustees to pass judgment on the parent's exercise of authority over his child.

This decision (reported in full in the *School Bulletin* for May, 1885) caused wide and generally unfavorable comment.

Superintendent Draper took a wholly different view, and gave to the author of this volume for publication a copy of the following letter, showing the ground afterward taken by the State department:

That the school authorities have the power to exclude from the benefits of the schools, pupils who refuse to comply with reasonable regulations relative to attendance, I have no doubt. I consider a regulation to the effect that a pupil who is absent or tardy shall bring his teacher a written excuse from his parent or guardian, to be entirely proper, and the department will therefore sustain you in enforcing it. The letter addressed to one of your teachers is a highly improper and insulting one. If this parent persists in sending his child to school with irregularity and in refusing to give any proper excuse for this course, you will be justified in excluding the child altogether.

The schools are surely for the benefit of all and all have common rights in them, but these rights must not be abused by any individual to the injury of others. If one parent can maintain the position which this one assumes, then *all* can, and if all can then the school system is liable to utter over-throw and destruction. This of course we cannot concede. You are advised to notify the person writing the letter which you enclose to me of the contents of this communication; to receive the child into the school if the parent manifests a disposition to comply with the law. Otherwise you will be upheld in excluding the child in question.

Here is a Missouri decision:

Suppose rule 11 to be inverted, and instead of reading as it now stands should read thus: "Any pupil is at liberty to go a-fishing during school hours and be absent a half day or a whole day and as many days as he pleases, provided he conducts himself decently when in attendance in school." And this is the point to which the argument of the plaintiff tends. The pupil, it is urged, is at liberty to be absent when he pleases, and such absence is a matter solely between him and his parents. But the studies in our public schools are, I presume, classified according to the ages and advancement of the scholars; and the continued or repeated absence of one of a class not only is injurious to the absentee, but if allowed beyond a certain point is calculated to demoralize those who attend, and damage the orderly instructions of the teacher. Taxes are not collected to pay teachers to sit in front of empty benches, or to hunt up truant boys. Such absences, when without excuse, are the fault of the parents, whose business it is to see that the attendance of their child is regular, unless prevented by causes which will, of course, be an excuse under the rule now in question.*

Vaccination.—Trustees and school boards are directed and empowered to exclude from the benefits of the common schools any child or person who has not been vaccinated, until such time when they shall become vaccinated. (Chap. xxv. General Laws.)

NOTE 1.—*Free vaccination.*—When such school board or trustees shall adopt a resolution to carry into effect this provision, they shall post in two or more public places in the district, at least 10 days' notice thereof, stating that due provision has been made for the vaccination of any child or person of suitable age who may desire to attend the common school, and whose parents or guardians are unable to procure vaccination for them. (Chap. xxv. General Laws.)

NOTE 2.—*Provisions.*—The trustees or board may appoint some competent physician and fix his compensation to be, with other necessary expenses, provided in the annual tax bill.

---

* 71 Mo. 628. See also 116 Mass. 366; 13 Brad. 520.

It shall be his duty to ascertain the number of children of school age who have not been vaccinated, and to furnish a list of the names of such to the trustees or school board; he shall provide himself with good and reliable vaccine virus wherewith to vaccinate such as have not been vaccinated, and to furnish to such certificates of vaccination when required. (Chap. xxv. General Laws.)

The compulsory law passed in 1894 requires that (*a*) every child between 14 and 16 not regularly employed, and (*b*) every child between 8 and 12, shall attend school as many days between Oct. 1 and June 1 as the public school shall be in session; and that (*c*) every child between 12 and 14 shall attend school upon at least 80 consecutive school days, and in addition upon all school days when not usefully employed.

NOTE 1.—Parents or guardians of children between 8 and 16 must cause such children to attend school, or give notice to the trustees of their inability to do so, under penalty of fine and imprisonment.

NOTE 2.—It is made unlawful to employ any child between 8 and 12 during the time the public school is in session; or to employ any child between 12 and 14 who does not present a certificate showing that the child has complied with the law respecting attendance, under penalty of fine.

NOTE 3.—Cities and union school districts shall appoint attendance officers to arrest children between 8 and 16 who are truants, and establish truant schools for children between 7 and 16 and confine habitual truants therein.

NOTE 4. One-half the State moneys may be withheld from any city or union school district neglecting to enforce the provisions of this act. But as the truant officer and the truant school are essential to its working, not much result can be expected from it in country district schools, except so far as Note 1 may be used to persuade parents to enforce their children's attendance, and Note 2 to prevent employers from giving work to pupils who should be in school.

(*b*) COURSE OF STUDY.—Trustees have the power to select the branches to be taught, and to require pupils to pursue them (*605, 606*).

NOTE 1.—Pupils must be instructed in physiology and hygiene, with special reference to the effects of alcoholic drinks, stimulants, and narcotics

(vii. 47. 11; xv. 19). Instruction in manual training may be prescribed (xv. 25), and advanced studies may be introduced (*621*).

NOTE 2.—Instruction in free-hand drawing must be given in all cities: and in all union school districts unless excused by the superintendent (xv. 21). Evening schools for this purpose may be established when directed by the city authorities, or by district meeting (xv. 22). Vocal music may be taught in cities and in union schools (xv. 23). Kindergartens may be established in cities, or in villages employing a superintendent (xv. 24).

Text-books.—In district schools, the text-books to be used are to be designated at any annual meeeting by a two-thirds vote of all the legal voters present and voting, and may not be changed within 5 years except by a three-fourths vote of those present and voting at an annual meeting.

In union free schools, the board of education adopts the text-books, and no change can be made within 5 years of adoption except by a three-fourths vote of the board (xv. 9, 10).

Changing text-books.—Any person superseding a text-book adopted for use in any public school by the board of education in cities, villages, and union free school districts, or in other district schools by a two-thirds vote of any annual meeting, within 5 years thereafter, except on a three-fourths vote of such board of education or annual district meeting, shall be liable to a penalty of not less than $50 nor more than $100, to be sued for by any tax-payer before any justice of the peace for the benefit of the district (xv. 11).

Religious exercises.—In New York it has been uniformly ruled that pupils cannot be compelled to attend religious services, and that the law gives no authority, as a matter of right, to use any portion of the regular school hours in conducting any religious exercises at which the attendance of pupils is made compulsory (*618–622*).

NOTE 1.—Some places, like the cities of Troy and Rochester, have forbidden any religious exercises. But in most communities opening the school with Bible-reading and some form of prayer is considered unobjectable and desirable.

It is the rule of the State department never to interfere in this matter unless some one in the community feels sufficiently aggrieved to appeal to the superintendent, in which case the law forbidding religious exercises in school hours is immediately enforced.

NOTE 2.—The practice of the department is the same with regard to the drawing of public money by Catholic schools. In some cities and villages, schools conducted by Sisters wearing the usual garb of their order are admitted under the public school system, the teachers being examined by local officers, and drawing pay from the public funds. This the superintendent permits except where his attention is officially called to it by regular appeal, in which case he is obliged to decide that such are not properly public schools and cannot participate in the public money (*622-625*).

NOTE 3.—It has been held that Catholic children could be expelled for non-attendance on days when their church compelled attendance upon religious exercises;* and in 1875 a Hebrew girl was expelled from the Sherwin school, Boston, for not attending the Saturday sessions. But the modern current of decisions is the other way, and trustees are advised to respect the religious observances of their pupils so far as the welfare of the school permits.

(*c*) CONDUCT OF PUPILS.—According to decisions in New York, the authority of trustees over pupils ceases with the close of school and their departure from the school premises (*602*).

NOTE 1.—The rule in other States is generally that the authority of the trustees is absolute on the school premises, and concurrent with the parent on the road home.†

NOTE 2.—A pupil may not be expelled for wearing her hair in a way disapproved of by the trustees (602).

---

* 48 Vt. 444.

† 31 Ia. 568; 8 Cush. 160; 32 Vt. 114.

(12) Give to teachers for their wages orders on the supervisor, or on the collector or the treasurer for the public moneys, so far as they are in their hands; and collect the rest of the wages by direct tax, but not to exceed four months in advance (vii. 47. 12).

NOTE 1.—It is a misdemeanor to give an order upon the supervisor, collector or treasurer unless there shall be on hand sufficient moneys belonging to the district to meet the same (vii. 47. 12, 15).

NOTE 2.—They may raise this tax even when it has not been voted by the district (vii. 47. 12).

NOTE 3.—The order can be drawn only in favor of the teacher. If he desires to apply the proceeds to the payment of a private debt, for board or other consideration, he can endorse it to his creditor, but it is for him and not for the trustees to distribute his wages (*400, 704, 707, 708*).

NOTE 4.—A contract compelling the teacher to board with the trustee is null and void (*597*).

NOTE 5.—No order shall be given for wages till the teacher has verified the school report (vii. 53; *427*).

Payment of unqualified teacher.—Trustees commit a misdemeanor by paying an unqualified teacher from the public moneys, or moneys raised by district tax, and any fines imposed on them shall be for the benefit of the schools of the county (vii. 40).

(13) Divide the public moneys into as many portions as there are terms, and raise the needed additional tax by terms (vii. 47. 13).

(14) Draw upon the supervisor, collector, or treasurer for the school and library money (vii. 47. 14). See iii. 4. 1, 2.

(15) After having paid toward teachers' wages

the public moneys applicable, raise the rest by tax (vii. 47. 15; *402, 403*).

Allowance.—In case a district shall have been excluded from its share of the public money by omitting to make any report (ii. 15), or to comply with any other requirements, if it shall be shown to the superintendent that such omission was accidental or excusable, he may make such district an equitable allowance (ii. 8).

Loss of school money.—The loss of any school moneys to a district through wilful neglect of duty by any school officer, renders such person liable for the whole amount with interest (xv. 1).

(16) Call special meetings, when requested by a respectable number of inhabitants (*565–568, 584, 742, 743*).

(17) Sue for and recover any moneys in the hands of any former trustees and apply the same to the use of the district (vii. 58).

(19) *Outbuildings.*—They shall provide at least two suitable water-closets or privies for every school under their charge, entirely separated from each other, and having separate means of access; the approaches thereto shall be separated by a substantial close fence not less than 7 feet in height (vii. 48; *269*).

NOTE 1.—It is the duty of such officers to keep these buildings in a clean and wholesome condition; and if they fail to comply with these requirements, it shall be sufficient ground for their removal from office, and the withholding from the district of any share of the public money (vii. 48).

NOTE 2.—Any tax to provide for the expenses thereof may be levied without a vote of the district when such expense shall have been approved by the school commissioner (vii. 48). The expense for the erection of necessary out-buildings when the district is unprovided with them, and the commissioner or superintendent has directed that they be built, is limited afterward to $50 (vii. 50). But no limit is placed to the expenditure to abate nuisances under direction of the commissioner (vii. 50).

(19) *Purchase of apparatus.*—Trustees may expend, without a vote of the district, a sum not to exceed $50 a year for necessary and proper repairs of the schoolhouse; and a sum not to exceed $25 a year for a dictionary, maps, globes and other school apparatus (vii. 50; *193*).

NOTE.—Trustees may also provide fuel, stoves, or other heating apparatus, pails, brooms, etc., when not voted by the district (vii. 50).

(20) *Libraries.*—The trustees shall appoint a teacher of the schools under their charge as librarian, who with the trustees shall be responsible for the safety and proper care of the books, and make such reports as the superintendent requires (xiii. 2).

NOTE.—Any books or other library property which have not been in direct charge of a librarian duly appointed within one year may be taken and shall be hereafter owned by any public library under State supervision which has received permission from the regents (xiii. 6).

No portion of the library money (see page 11) shall be expended except for books approved by the superintendent: which shall consist of (*a*) reference books for use in the schoolroom; (*b*) suitable supplementary reading books for children; (*c*) books relating to branches being pursued in the school; or (*d*) pedagogic books as aids to teachers (xiii. 1).

NOTE 1.—All districts may raise money by tax for their libraries, or receive gifts or bequests to maintain them (xiii. 4).

NOTE 2.—It is not necessary that the approval of the superintendent be secured before the purchase of the books, but the books must be such that he is likely to approve of. A list of suitable books may be obtained from the publisher of this volume.

The library is to be a part of the school equipment and kept in the school building at all times; but teachers, school officers, and pupils may borrow not more than one at a time of the volumes not needed for reference, and keep the same not to exceed two weeks (xiii. 2).

NOTE.—The board of education in a city or union free school district, or the school meeting in an ordinary district may give all its books to any township or other free public library under State supervision, provided it is free to such city or district (xiii. 5).

(21) *Branch schools.*—Whenever necessary, the trustees may open branch schools at the expense of the district (vii. 50; *598*).

(22) *Contracts with city schools.*—Trustees may be empowered by majority vote of the district to make written contract with the board of education of an adjoining city or village of not less than 6,000 inhabitants to permit the children of such district to be taught in the schools of such city, and such district shall receive its district quota (xv. 14).

(23) *Records.*—The trustees shall keep in a blank book a record of all movable property belonging to the district, and their accounts of moneys received and expended. In another the teachers shall keep a record of all the pupils attending school, their ages, etc., and until the teacher has verified the entries by

oath the trustees shall not give an order for wages (vii. 53; *427*).

Payment to themselves.—Trustees cannot receive pay for their services *as trustees* (*750*) and must not employ themselves as teachers (*744*, *765*). They may receive pay for services as workmen for the district (*745*), but should submit to the district meeting the allowance for such services (*752*) or for any material furnished by them (*750*). They may employ a person to do the clerical work in making out the tax-list (*756*).

(24) *Reports.*—Shall, on the 1st day of August in each year, make in writing a report to the school commissioner, and deliver the same to the town clerk (vii. 59; *203–215*, *763*). Shall also once a year make full reports to the district (vii. 53, 55; *203–215*, *763*), and when their office expires pay to their successors all unexpended district moneys (vii. 56).

Failure to make report.—Any trustee refusing or neglecting to render an annual account of moneys received and paid shall forfeit any unexpired term of office, and become liable to the trustees for any district moneys in his hands (vii. 57).

UNION FREE SCHOOLS

Establishment.—When 15 persons entitled to vote at any district meeting shall sign a call for a meeting to determine the establishment of a union free school in the district, it shall be the duty of the trustees within 10 days after the call shall be presented to them to give such public notice as is required by law that a meeting of the inhabitants will be held for such purpose at a suitable place, and at a time not less than 20 nor more than 30 days thereafter (viii. 1).

Union meeting.—When 15 such persons from each of two or more adjoining districts, shall unite in a call for a meeting of the inhabitants of such districts, to determine whether the districts shall be consolidated by the establishment of a union free school therein, it shall be the duty of the trustees of those districts, or a majority of them, to give the notice as above for a meeting to be held within the districts at some convenient place (viii. 4; *776–780*).

NOTE 1.—When such district corresponds wholly or in part with an incorporated village, the notice shall be published once a week for 3 consecutive weeks before the meeting in all the newspapers in the district, and at least 5 copies shall be posted conspicuously in said district 20 days prior to the meeting (viii. 2).

NOTE 2.—In other districts the notice shall be thus posted, and the trustees shall require some taxable inhabitant to notify every other taxable inhabitant (viii. 2).

NOTE 3.—The expense of these notices shall be borne by the district if the union free school is established, but if not, by the inhabitants signing the call (viii. 3).

NOTE 4.—The qualifications of voters are the same as at district meetings (vii. 11; viii. 8. See page 20.)

NOTE 5.—When one or more districts adjoin a union free school district whose limits do not correspond with those of an incorporated village or city, the commissioner may upon written consent of the trustees of all the districts affected dissolve such district or districts, and annex the territory to the union free school district (viii. 30).

Election of trustees.—Whenever any such meeting, or any adjournment thereof for a period not longer than 10 days from a previous meeting, at which not less than 15 persons entitled to vote thereat shall, by the affirmative vote of a majority present and voting, determine to establish a union free school in said district, it shall be lawful for such meeting to proceed to the election by ballot of not less than 3 nor more than 9 trustees, in place of the existing trustees, whose terms shall cease when the others assume office, for a board of education (viii. 5).

NOTE 1.—Copies of the call for, and the minutes of meetings, duly certified by the chairman and secretary thereof, shall be by them transmitted to and deposited with the town clerk, the school commissioner, and the superintendent, respectively (viii. 5).

NOTE 2.—If it shall be decided not to establish a union free school, no other meeting for such purpose shall be called within a year thereafter. Nor shall a union free school district thus formed be dissolved within the period of one year from the first Tuesday of August following such meeting (viii. 5). For proceedings for dissolution, see viii. 32-42.

NOTE 3.—Neither a supervisor nor a school commissioner may be a member of a board of education, and a member elected to either of these offices vacates his office as a member (viii. 5). Compare vii. 22.

NOTE 4.—The trustees so elected shall be, by order of such meeting, divided into three classes to serve one, two, and three years respectively (viii. 9).

NOTE 5.—When the limits of such constituted district correspond with those of any incorporated city or village, their term of service shall be computed from the date of the next charter election in such city or village, and new members shall be elected at such annual elections thereafter, in place of those whose terms expire (viii. 6). In other districts their term of service shall be completed the first Tuesday of August following (viii. 5; *769*).

Change in number of members.—The qualified voters may determine by a majority vote to increase or diminish the number of members of the board of education, but no board shall consist of fewer than 3 or more than 9 members (viii. 31).

Dissolution.—It shall be the duty of the board of

education of any union free school district, established not less than one year (viii. 5), upon the application of 15 resident taxpayers of the district, to call a special meeting, in the manner prescribed by law, for the purpose of determining whether application shall be made for the dissolution of such district, and its reorganization as a common school district or districts (viii. 32).

NOTE 1.—*Re-division into districts.*—If such dissolved district shall have been established by the consolidation of two or more districts, it shall be lawful for the commissioner to direct that its territory be divided to correspond as far as practicable, with the districts that were consolidated (viii. 34).

NOTE 2.—*Time for annual meeting.*—The annual meeting shall be held in the district or districts, after the dissolution, on the first Tuesday of August, and officers shall be elected as required by law (viii. 38).

NOTE 3.—*Report to superintendent.*—It shall be the duty of the board of education of the district affected forthwith to furnish the superintendent copies of the call, notice, proceedings of the meeting, and proceedings of the commissioner taken thereon (viii. 40).

NOTE 4.—*Not to be repeated within 3 years.*—Whenever, at such meeting, it shall be determined by a majority vote not to dissolve such district, or if the school commissioner shall not approve the proceedings of such meeting, no other meeting for a similar purpose shall be held in the district within 3 years from the time the first meeting was held (viii. 33, 39).

Notice to commissioner.—If it shall be determined by a two-thirds vote of the legal voters, as above, to dissolve such district, it shall be the duty of the board of education to present to the school commissioner a certified copy of the call, notice, and proceedings. If he shall approve of the proceedings of such meeting, he shall certify the same to the board of education; and on the day preceding the first Tuesday of August next thereafter such district shall cease to be a union free school district (viii. 33).

Annual meeting.—The annual school meeting of a union free school district when limits do not correspond with those of an incorporated village or city shall be on the first Tuesday of August (viii. 13). In districts whose limits correspond with those of an incorported village, the election shall be by separate ballot at the charter election (viii. 6).

NOTE 1.—The meeting has the right to choose its own chairman (*784*).

NOTE 2.—*Meetings of the board of education.*—In either case, the annual meeting of the new board of education for organization shall be on the Tuesday following the election (viii. 13), and there must be regular meetings at least four times a year (viii. 22). Such meetings are open to the public, but executive sessions may be held open only to the board and persons invited to be present (viii. 22).

Clerk.—There shall be elected at each annual meeting a clerk of the district and of the board of education (*776*). He must be a qualified voter of the district, not a trustee or a teacher employed in the district (viii. 7), and able to read and write (viii. 8).

NOTE 1.—This section does not affect the towns of Cortlandt and White Plains, in Westchester county (viii. 42).

NOTE 2.—In case the annual meeting fails to elect, the board of education shall appoint one of their own number to act as clerk (viii 7).

NOTE 3.—The board have power also to appoint one of the taxable inhabitants of the district treasurer, and another as collector of the moneys raised, to hold office during the pleasure of the board; each shall execute and deliver a bond to the board, of a sufficient security, within 10 days after written notice of his appointment shall have been duly served upon him (viii. 7; *769, 770, 771*).

POWERS OF A BOARD OF EDUCATION.—The board of education is:

(1) To adopt by-laws and rules for its own government (viii. 15. 1).

Trustees have this power by implication.

(2) To establish such rules and regulations concerning the order and discipline of the schools as they may deem necessary to secure the best educational results (viii. 15. 2).

Here their powers are the same as those of trustees. See pages 37–45.

(3) To prescribe the course of study, and regulate the admission and transfer of pupils (viii. 15. 3; 28).

These are the powers of trustees. See pages 43–45; 37, 38.

NOTE 1.—The board of education adopts the text-books, however, while trustees must refer the matter to the district meeting. See page 44.

NOTE 2.—*Colored children.*—In cities and incorporated villages, and in union schools or schools under special act when authorized by district vote, the board may establish separate schools for colored children (xv. 28–30; *514*).

(4) To prescribe the text-books used, and compel uniformity in the use of the same; and to furnish the same to pupils out of any moneys provided for the purpose (viii. 15. 4).

In ordinary districts the school meeting adopts the text-books; in union free school districts, this power is vested in the board of education (*737*). See page 44.

In ordinary districts text-books can be furnished only to indigent pupils. See page 23. In union free school districts they may be furnished to all pupils if the district provides the money.

(5) To make provision for the instruction of pupils

in physiology and hygiene with reference to the effects of stimulants and narcotics (viii. 15. 5).

This is also required of trustees. See page 43.

(6) (*a*) To purchase sites as designated by a district meeting (ix. 5); (*b*) to construct such schoolhouses as may be designated; (*c*) to purchase furniture and apparatus; (*d*) to keep the schoolhouse and furniture in repair; (*e*) to hire rooms for the school when needed; (*f*) to insure the schoolhouse and contents (viii. 15. 6).

(*a, b*) *To purchase sites and construct schoolhouses.*—Here the duties of the board are the same as those of trustees. See page 32.

NOTE.—*In cities of more than 30,000*, except in the city of Brooklyn (ix. 4), it shall not be lawful under the "condemnation law" (title 1, of chapter 23, of the Code of Civil Procedure) to acquire less than the whole of any city or village lot; or any premises occupied as a homestead without consent of the owner; or beyond the corporate limits of the city any garden or orchard or manufacturing establishment without consent of the owner (ix. 2).

Villages and cities.—In incorporated cities and villages, the corporate authorities shall from time to time raise by tax such sums as are set forth in a written statement in detail, and declared by the board of education to be necessary, for purposes of anticipated expenditures; and such authorities have no power to withhold the sums declared to be necessary for teachers' wages and the ordinary contingent expenses of the school. They shall also raise such further sums as may have been voted at the district meeting for sites, buildings, and apparatus (viii. 9),

Districts not villages.—In districts whose limits do not correspond with those of an incorporated city or village, a majority of the voters present at any annual or special district meeting, properly called, may authorize such acts and vote such taxes as they shall deem expedient for the support and welfare of the school (viii. 9).

In union free school districts the commissioner's approval of the tax or of the plan of ventilation is not required (*783*). See page 23 (8), Note 1. There is no limit to the amount that may be raised (*782*, *783*).

NOTE 1.—No addition to or change of site or purchase of a new site, or tax for the purchase of any new site or structure, or for the purchase of an addition to the site of any schoolhouse, or for building any new schoolhouse, or for the erection of an addition to any schoolhouse, shall be voted by such meeting unless a notice by the board of education stating that such tax will be proposed and specifying the amount and object thereof, shall have been published each week for the four weeks next preceding the meeting in two newspapers published in the district, or in one paper if there be but one published; if no newspaper be published in the district, the said notice shall be posted in at least 10 of the most public places in the district for 20 days before the meeting (viii. 9).

NOTE 2.—No vote to raise money shall be rescinded, nor the amount thereof be reduced, unless the same be done within 10 days after the sum has been first voted (viii. 9).

NOTE 3.—The money so voted may be levied in one sum or by instalments. When by instalments the corporate authorities are authorized to borrow so much as may be necessary at a rate of interest not exceeding 6 per cent (vii. 9).

NOTE 4.—All moneys for teachers' wages, after the due application of the school moneys thereto, shall be raised by tax (viii. 11).

(c) *To purchase furniture and apparatus.*—In ordinary districts, the expenditure of the trustees without vote of the district is limited to $25 for apparatus. See page 48.

(*d*) *To keep the schoolhouse and furniture in repair.*—In ordinary districts, the expenditure of the trustees without vote of the district is limited to $50. See page 48. In union free school districts there is no limit.

NOTE.—This does not however authorize material additions to the school property, or the adoption of an expensive system of heating or ventilation (*776*), which should be by vote of the district.

(*e*) *To hire rooms for the school when needed.*—Trustees have the same authority. See page 48.

(*f*) *To insure the schoolhouse and contents.*—Trustees have the same power, if the district neglects to authorize it. See page 33.

(7) To hold the property of the district in charge (viii. 15. 7).

Trustees have the same power. See page 32.

(8) To sell property of the district, when authorized by vote (viii. 15. 8).

Trustees have the same authority (vii. 20). See page 32.

(9) To take and hold any gift or legacy to the district (viii. 15. 9).

In ordinary districts this is one of the duties of the supervisor (*593*).

(10) (*a*) To have the superintendence, management, and control of the school; (*b*) to establish in the same an academical department when warranted, or, when authorized by the district, to adopt an established academy as the academic department (viii.

27); (*c*) to receive non-resident pupils, and establish tuition-fees; (*d*) to provide fuel, furniture, and other necessaries for the school; and (*e*) to appoint librarians (viii. 15. 10).

(*a*) *To have the superintendence, management, and control of the school.*—This is identical with the power of trustees to establish rules and regulations. See pages 37–45.

(*b*) *To establish an academic department*—(viii. 27). This is a power denied to ordinary districts (*771*).

Requirements.—Such academic department shall be under visitation of the regents, and subject in its course of education and matters pertaining thereto to their rules (viii. 26).

Grading of schools.—The following system of grading has been adopted by the regents.

(1) The name *high school* shall be limited to schools giving a full four-year course, and supported by taxation, and the name *academy* to schools giving a similar course, not so supported.

(2) The academic departments of public schools giving less than a four-year course shall be graded as *junior*, *middle* and *senior* schools, according as they give *one*, *two* or *three*-year academic courses.

NOTE.—Schools not supported by taxation and giving academic courses of less than four years shall be similarly graded as *junior*, *middle* and *senior academic* schools.

(3) Such schools shall be admitted on a minimum of $200, $300, or $400 respectively for books, and

on the provision of such apparatus as is required for teaching the subjects in the courses adopted.

NOTE 1.—Only full years shall be counted in grading.

NOTE 2.—The grade shall be determined not by courses offered in the catalogue, but by instruction really given to one or more students during the course. Studies may be counted if each student during his course has full opportunity to take them, though not given each year.

NOTE 3.—No school shall be admitted to the university unless its course of instruction includes at least 12 counts or one full year of academic work.

NOTE 4.—Secondary schools of the university shall be classified by this system on their own report of instruction for the present year, and this grading shall be revised by the inspectors at each visit. Every school below junior grade shall be notified that it will be dropped from the university roll if it does not meet the minimum conditions by January 1, 1896.

NOTE 5.—Each junior school shall be at liberty to select for its course any 12 academic counts covered by the regents' examinations.

Form of application.—The following is the form prescribed :

To the regents of the University of the State of New York:

The undersigned, the board of education of the union school of ...., county of ...., respectfully represent :

That said union school has been established under the provisions of chapter 555 of the laws of 1864; that an academic department has been organized and is in operation in said school; and that the said academic department occupies the building appropriated to said school [or a separate building provided for its use]; that a suitable library and apparatus have been provided, as shown by the following description of grounds and buildings, and list of library and apparatus. [*Give as directed in form furnished by the regents on application.*]

Therefore the undersigned hereby ask the regents to admit the said academic department to the University of the State of New York, according to the provisions of law. [*To be signed by the members of the board of education*]

Procedure.—As soon as practicable, any institution making application for admission will be visited by a regents' inspector, who will examine its equipment and advise with its officers as to plans for the future. Applications for charters or certificates of admission can, however, be forwarded at any time either before or after the inspector's visit and will, unless there be a special reason to the contrary, be acted on by the regents at their next meeting. If favorably considered, a certificate of admission will be granted.

Adoption of existing academy.—When an academy exists within a union free school district, the board of education may if authorized by a vote of the district, and with the consent of the trustees of the academy, adopt such academy as the academic department of the district. The board may lease such academy and site, and maintain an academic department therein (viii. 27).

NOTE.—If a union school district which has adopted an academy as an academic department be dissolved, the academy shall upon application of a majority of the surviving trustees or stockholders be transferred to them (viii. 35).

Registration.—The regents will authorize the inspection of any school of academic or higher grade which shall apply for the same, and which shall pay the total cost to the University of the inspector's time and travelling expenses.

The academic fund.—The sum of $12,000 from the income of the literature fund, $34,000 from that of the U. S. deposit fund, and $60,000 from the general fund is annually paid for the benefit of academies, according to apportionment made by regents' examinations held in such academies. (*Chap. 378, laws of 1892.*)

NOTE 1.—Of the $106,000 thus apportioned, $60,000 from the general fund may be used only for the academic departments of union schools.

NOTE 2.—*Provisional examinations.*—On evidence satisfactory to the office, preferably the recommendation of a regents' inspector, that the best educational interests of a school demand it, the privilege of taking regents' examinations for a period not to exceed one year is sometimes granted provisionally while the school authorities are completing the requirements necessary for full admission.

Certificates of diplomas earned at examinations provisionally granted as above do not draw money from the academic fund unless the school at which they are earned is admitted to the University before the apportionment of the academic fund is made for that year.

NOTE 3.—The moneys apportioned to common school districts must be applied to the departments below the academical; and all moneys from the literature fund or otherwise appropriated for the academical department, to the latter (viii. 23).

Reports.—The regents shall require of each academic department an annual report giving information concerning trustees, faculty, students, instruction, equipment, methods, and operations, etc.

NOTE.—For refusal to neglect to make this report, the regents may suspend its charter, or any of its rights and privileges.

Teachers' classes.—Such academies and union schools as are designated by the superintendent may instruct teachers' classes of not less than 10 or more than 25, for terms of not less than 16 weeks. For each such scholar the school shall receive $1.00 for each week's instruction (xi. 3).

NOTE 1.—The schools shall be chosen by the superintendent so as to distribute them among the commissioner districts, having reference to the number of school districts in each, and the location and character of the institutions (xi. 3).

NOTE 2.—The instruction must be free to the pupils in the class (xi. 4).

NOTE 3.—The superintendent shall prescribe the conditions of admission, the course of instruction, the rules and regulations under which it shall be given, the number of classes in a year, and the length of time exceeding 16 weeks during which instruction may be given (xi. 3).

NOTE 4.—At the close of the term, the commissioner shall examine said classes, and issue teachers' certificates to such as prove worthy (xi. 7).

(*c*) *To receive non-resident pupils.*—Trustees also have this power. See page 38.

(*d*) *To provide fuel, furniture and other necessaries.*—In ordinary districts, the expenditure of trustees without vote of the district is limited to the purchase of "fuel, stoves or other heating apparatus, pails, brooms and other implements necessary to keep the schoolhouse or houses and the school-room or rooms clean and to make them reasonably comfortable for use, when no provision therefor has been made by a vote by the district, or the sum voted by the district for said purpose shall have proved insufficent" (vii. 50). See page 48. The purchase of furniture by boards of education is already authorized by 6 (*c*), page 57.

(*e*) *To appoint librarians.*—Trustees have this power. See page 48.

(11) To employ by written contract, and to pay qualified teachers by written contract (viii. 15, 11). This power is the same as that of trustees. See pages 33–37.

NOTE.—The contract is subject to the rules established by the board (*774*).

(12) To fill any vacancies in the board (viii. 15. 12; *766*, *770*).

In ordinary districts vacancies are filled by the district meeting, or by the commissioner. See page 29.

(13) To remove a member of the board for official misconduct (viii. 15. 13; *768, 770*).

In ordinary districts, only the superintendent can remove a trustee. See page 29.

NOTE.—The superintendent may remove any member of a board, for cause shown and after given opportunity for defence. Wilful violation or neglect of duty is cause for removal (viii. 29).

(14) To provide for the school at least two water-closets, entirely separated and with separate means of access (viii. 15. 14).

Trustees have this power, but it must be exercised under direction of the commissioner, and the amount must not exceed $50. See pages 47, 48.

(15) To build outside stairways on buildings more than two stories high (viii. 15. 15).

This is also required of trustees. See page 31.

(16) If the population of the district is more than 5,000, and if it is thought advisable, to appoint a superintendent (viii. 17). See page 18.

Trustees of a large district school might appoint head teacher and call him superintendent; but he would not draw the $800; and he would have to hold a teacher's certificate, which is not required of city and village superintendents.

(17) To keep an accurate record of its proceedings in books open to public inspection (viii. 18).

This is also required of trustees. See page 49.

(18) To publish each year 20 days before the annual meeting in at least one newspaper of the district a detailed account of all moneys received and expended (viii. 18).

This is not required of trustees.

(19) To appoint committees to visit all schools at least twice in each quarter, and report at the next regular meeting (viii. 22).

This is not required of trustees.

(20) To appoint an attendance officer for the arrest of truants (*Chap. 671, laws of 1894*). See page 43.

NOTE.—They may establish schools or set apart separate rooms for truant schools (*Chap. 671, laws of 1894*).

(21) *Drawing.*—To cause free instruction to be given in free-hand or industrial drawing, unless excused by the superintendent (xv. 21).

This is not required of trustees, though it is of course permitted. See page 43.

NOTE.—Boards are also authorized to maintain evening schools for instruction in industrial drawing, whenever the city authorizes in a city, or the district meeting in other union free school districts, shall so vote, for which purpose additional power to raise money for this purpose is conferred (xv. 22).

(22) *Vocal music.*—Boards may cause free instruction to be given in vocal music (xv. 23).

Trustees no doubt have the same power under their general control of the course of study (page 43); but this is a special authorization, meant to encourage the study of music.

(23) *Kindergartens.*—Boards may establish and maintain one or more kindergarten schools (xv. 24).

Trustees have no such power. See page 44.

NOTE 1.—No child under 4 years may be admitted, and the board may fix the highest limit of age. Children under 5 years shall be reported separately, and shall not be counted in distributing the public moneys (xv. 24).

NOTE 2.—All teachers employed in these kindergartens must be licensed like other teachers (see page 33); and are counted in the district quotas (see page 10).

(24) *Industrial training.*—Boards may maintain departments of industrial training; and purchase such outfit and employ such teachers as may be authorized by the city authorities or district meeting (xv. 25).

Trustees have the same power. See page 44.

(25) *Colored children.*—Boards in any city or incorporated village, and other union free schools when authorized by district meeting, may establish separate but equal schools for children of African descent (xv. 28, 29).

Trustees have no such power. See page 38.

(26) *Orphan asylums.*—The schools of the incorporated orphan asylum societies, except in the city of New York, shall participate in the public moneys, and shall be subject to the rules and regulations of the school authorities in their respective districts, but shall remain under the immediate management and direction of the said societies (xv. 32).

(27) *Arbor day.*—It shall be the duty of the authorities of every public school to assemble the

scholars on the Friday following the 1st day of May, to conduct such exercises as shall tend to encourage the planting, protection, and preservation of trees and shrubs (xv. 45).

NOTE—Pamphlets containing a course of exercises and instruction are published and distributed annually by the superintendent (xv. 46).

(28) To keep within the appropriation in all expenditures (viii. 23).

NOTE.—In the union schools of cities or incorporated villages, all moneys appropriated or raised by tax are to be paid into the city or village treasury, and kept distinct; and no money can be drawn from these funds except by resolution of the board, and by drafts signed by the president and countersigned by the secretary or clerk stating on their face the purpose for which they are issued (viii. 24).

NOTE 2.—In other union schools, the said funds shall be paid to the treasurers of the boards of education, and money drawn only by resolution and draft as in Note 1. In these districts, the boards shall annually render to the school commissioner accounts of all moneys received and expended, with every voucher, and certified copies of every order of the board (viii. 25).

Estimate of money required.—At the annual meeting of the district, the board shall present, besides any other report or statement required by law, a detailed statement in writing of the amount of money required for the ensuing year for school purposes, exclusive of the public moneys, specifying the several purposes for which it will be required and the amount of each. When demanded by any voter present, the question of voting the necessary taxes shall be taxed upon each item separately, and the inhabitants may increase or reduce any estimated expenditures, except those for teachers' wages and the ordinary contingent expenses of the school (viii. 18, 19). Compare report of trustees, page 50.

Taxation without vote.—If the inhabitants shall neglect or refuse to vote the sums estimated necessary for teachers' wages after applying thereto the public moneys, and the moneys received or to be received for that purpose, or shall refuse or neglect to vote the sums estimated necessary for contingent expenses, the board may levy a tax for the same in like manner as if it had been voted by the inhabitants (viii. 20).

Trustees have power to levy tax for teachers' wages, but not for the contingent expenses of the school except within the limits already specified for insurance, fuel, repairs, etc. See pages 33, 47, 48.

NOTE.—The board may not levy this tax unless the limit has been presented at an annual or special meeting, and the inhabitants have neglected or refuse to vote it (*783*).

(29) To exercise, except as specially provided for above, all the powers and duties of school trustees (ix. 3; *768*); and whenever an academic department is established, of trustees of academies (viii. 16; chap. 378, laws of 1892).

DISTRICT AND UNION FREE SCHOOLS COMPARED.—The principal differences between district and union free schools may be summarized as follows:

(*a*) *Powers exercised by trustees with restriction; by boards of education without restriction.*

1. To purchase apparatus. Pages 48, 57.
2. To repair schoolhouses and furniture. Pages 48, 58.
3. To provide fuel, furniture, and other necessaries. Pages 48, 63.

4. To build outhouses. Pages 47, 48, 64.

(*b*) *Powers exercised in ordinary districts by the district meeting; in union free school districts by the board of education.*

1. To prescribe text-books. Pages 44, 55.
2. To purchase furniture. Pages 48, 57, 63.
3. To turn over the library to a public library. Page 49.
4. To fill vacancies in the board. Pages 29, 63.
5. To waive relationship of teacher to trustee. Page 34.

(*c*) *Powers exercised by boards of education that do not exist in ordinary districts.*

1. To hold gifts and legacies. Page 58.
2. To remove members of the board. Pages 29, 64.
3. To appoint a superintendent. Pages 18, 64.
4. To publish an annual financial statement in a newspaper. Page 65.
5. To appoint visiting committees. Page 65.
6. To levy without vote of district a tax for contingent expenses. Pages 33, 47, 48, 56, 66.
7. To appoint an attendance officer. Pages 43, 65.
8. To establish truant schools. Pages 43, 65.
9. To establish kindergartens. Pages 44, 67.

(*d*) *Powers of the school-meeting in union free school districts that do not exist in ordinary districts.*

1. To provide free text-books. Pages 23, 55.
2. To vote a tax for a schoolhouse without limit or approval of commissioner. Pages 31, 57.
3. To establish an academical department. Page 59.
4. To raise money for evening drawing-schools. Page 67.
5. To establish separate schools for colored children. Pages 38, 66.

(30) To make on Aug. 1 of each year and deposit in the town clerk's office a report to the commissioner of all matters on which trustees are required to report (see page 49), and on such other matters as the superintendent may require (viii. 28 ; *769*).

NOTE.—Every union school is subject to the visitation of the superintendent, who has general supervision over the board of education and the management and conduct of the departments of instruction. He may at any time require of the board a report upon any particular matter (viii. 28). Wilful disodedience of any lawful requirement of the superintendent is cause for removal (viii. 29). Any person may appeal to the superintendent against the action of any special meeting or the order of a commissioner altering or dissolving a union free school district (viii. 41).

NORMAL SCHOOLS

New State normal schools are now established only by vote of the legislature.

Local boards.—The immediate supervision and management of each normal school, subject to the general supervision and direction of the superintendent, is vested in its local board, the members of which are appointed by the superintendent for life, subject only to removal by the concurrent action of the superintendent and of the chancellor of the university of the State of New York.

Management.—These boards (*a*) make the rules and regulations; (*b*) make annual reports to the legislature on Jan. 1; (*c*) prescribe the course of instruction; and (*d*) employ the teachers: their action being in all these matters subject to the approval of the superintendent.

NOTE.—The superintendent determines how many teachers shall be employed, and their salaries.

Course of Study.—Normal schools must give instruction (*a*) in physiology and hygiene, with special reference to the effects of alcoholic drinks, stimulants, and narcotics (xv. 19); (*b*) in industrial and free-hand drawing (xv. 21); (*c*) in vocal music (xv. 23); (*d*) in industrial training so far as prescribed by the superintendent and their local boards (xv. 27);

They are entitled to receive from the American Museum of Natural History, at least one illustrated lecture every year, and such appliances, plates, and apparatus as may be necessary for proper instruction in natural history (Chap. 428, laws of 1886; chap. 6, laws of 1893).

Pupils.—The statute provides for proportionate representation of the counties, but in practice any pupil in the State may select which normal school he will attend. They are admitted upon recommendation of a school commissioner or city superintendent, approved by the superintendent, and upon passing an examination.

NOTE.—The examination questions from 1887 to 1892 are published in "The New York Question Book", with "Supplement No. 1" and "Supplement No. 2."

Expenses.—Pupils are entitled to all the privileges of the school, free from charges for tuition, or for the use of books or apparatus.

NOTE 1.—Pupils not residents of the State must pay tuition.

NOTE 2.—The pupil's railroad fare from home to the school one way each term is paid by the State.

Academic departments.—Normal schools cannot receive into their academic departments any pupil not a resident of the territory for the benefit of which the State has pledged itself to maintain such department (Chap. 142, laws of 1889).

NOTE.—This applies to the schools which turned over academic property to the State on certain conditions.

Tuition money received by normal schools may be used for current expenses (Chap. 492, laws of 1870).

INDIAN SCHOOLS

Management.—These are in charge of the superintendent, who shall establish such schools as he thinks necessary, employ superintendents, and, with the concurrence of the comptroller and secretary of State, cause to be erected the necessary buildings (xv. 33).

Public moneys.—Indian children between 4 and 21 shall draw public money the same as white children, and such money must be exclusively devoted to their education (xv. 36). There shall also be an annual appropriation of $6,000 by the legislature (xv. 37). See page 10.

INSTITUTIONS FOR THE DEAF AND DUMB, AND FOR THE BLIND.

Management.—These institutions are subject to the visitation of the superintendent (xv. 40).

Admission.—All deaf and dumb or blind persons, resident of this State for the three years preceding, upwards of 12 years of age, shall be eligible to appointment as State pupils to one of the institutions in this State. Such appointments are made by the superintendent, upon application under such conditions as to share of expense to be paid by parents, guardians, or friends as he may impose (xv. 41; *131–138*).

NOTE.—Appointments to the Institution for the Blind in Batavia are not made by the superintendent.

CORNELL SCHOLARSHIPS

NOTE—In bestowing upon Cornell University, as an endowment, the public lands granted this State by congress in 1862, the State reserved the privileges of free instruction to be given to a limited number of pupils from all parts of the State at such institution.

Number.—The institution shall annually receive students to the number of one from each assembly district in the State, free of tuition fees or incidental charges (xii. 1).

NOTE.—In case a candidate entitled to the scholarship by reason of highest standing in the examination should fail in his entrance examination at the university, should die, resign, be expelled, or vacate such scholarship in any way, either before or after entering, then the candidate next in excellence becomes entitled to it; if there be no such candidate resident in the county, then the superintendent may appoint one from some other county (xii. 1. 5).

How awarded.—These scholarships shall be awarded by competitive examination of candidates by the school commissioners and city superintendents of each county. These examinations shall occur at the court-house of each county on the first Saturday in June in each year. The questions are prepared by the department of Public Instruction and the examination papers handed in are to be forwarded there (xii. 1).

NOTE 1.—The questions from the beginning to 1892 are published in "The New York Question Book", and in "Supplement No. 1", and "Supplement No. 2."

NOTE 2.—As it is intended that this free instruction shall be a reward for superior scholarship in the public schools, none are eligible but those who have attended some of the common schools or academies of the State at least 6 months of the year immediately preceeding the examination, and who are at least 16 years of age (xii. 1. 2). Children of those who have died in the military or naval service of the United States are to have preference (xii. 1. 7).

NOTE 3.—A student may in the discretion of the president of the university be granted leave of absence from his studies for the purpose of earning funds to defray his living expenses at school, and be allowed 6 years to complete the course (xii. 1. 6).

THE UNIVERSITY OF THE STATE OF NEW YORK

NOTE.—The present university law is chapter 378, of the laws of 1892.

History.—The university of the State of New York was created in 1784 under the name of "regents of the university of the State of New York", as a branch of the State government.

NOTE.—The word "regent" was first used by the University of Paris, and signified a master qualified to teach. In the English universities the rule grew up that only those masters actually teaching, the "regents" as distinguished from the non-regents, should have a right to vote in certain university assemblies, the regent combining the functions of teaching and of governing. New York put the name to a new use, making the regents not the teaching but the governing body.—*Sidney Sherwood's History, pages 256, 257.*

The objects of the university are to encourage and promote higher education; to visit and inspect its several institutions and departments; to distribute to or expend or administer for them such property and funds as the State may appropriate therefor, or as the university may own or hold in trust or otherwise; etc.

NOTE.—In 1812 it started the movement that resulted in forming the system of public instruction; in 1833 it established teachers' classes; in 1864 it started its system of examinations; and in 1892 it received exclusive power of granting charters to educational institutions in the State. It has published annual reports, which since 1835 have given educational statistics in great detail. In 1863 it established the university convocation, an annual meeting of teachers which has grown to be one of the most important in the country. In 1889 it took up the work of university extension.

Extent.—The university consists of all institutions

of higher education which are now or may hereafter be incorporated in this State, and such other libraries, museums or other institutions for higher education as may, in conformity with the ordinances of the regents, after official inspection, be admitted to or incorporated by the university.

Government.—The university is governed and its corporate powers exercised by 23 regents, including the governor, lieutenant-governor, secretary of state, and superintendent, who are regents by virtue of their offices.

NOTE 1.—In case of the death, resignation, or removal from the State of any elective regent, his successor shall be chosen by the legislature in the manner provided by law for the election of senators in congress, except that the election may take place at any time during the session of the legislature as it may determine.

NOTE 2.—No person shall be at the same time a regent of the university and a trustee, president, principal, or any other officer of any institution belonging to the university.

Officers.—The elective officers of the university are a chancellor, a vice-chancellor, a secretary, and such other officers as are either authorized by law, or deemed necessary by the regents, all of whom are chosen by ballot and hold office during the pleasure of the regents.

NOTE.—No election, removal or change of salary of an elective officer shall be made by less than ten votes in favor thereof. Each officer so elected shall, before entering on his duties, take and file with the secretary of state the oath of office required of State officers.

Chancellor.—The chancellor presides at all meetings of the regents, confers all degrees which they shall authorize, and fixes the time and place of all special meetings.

NOTE.—In his absence the vice-chancellor, or, if he be also absent, the senior regent present, performs the duties and has all the powers of the chancellor.

Secretary.—The secretary is responsible for the safe-keeping and proper use of the university seal, and of the books, records, and other property in charge of the regents, and for the proper administration and discipline of its various offices and departments.

NOTE 1.—He shall give bonds, to be approved by the chancellor, in writing, in the penal sum of $10,000 for the faithful discharge of his duties.

NOTE 2.—He shall have power to appoint, subject to the confirmation of the chancellor, any other officer of the university as his deputy to exercise temporarily any specified powers of the secretary in his absence.

Meetings.—In addition to the annual meeting, the chancellor shall call a meeting as often as the business of the university requires, or if 5 regents in writing so request.

NOTE 1.—At least 10 days notice of every meeting shall be given to each regent. If any regent shall fail to attend the meetings for one year without written excuse accepted as satisfactory by the regents, he shall be deemed to have resigned, and the regents shall report the vacancy to the legislature if in session, or at the opening of its next succeeding session, when the vacancy must be filled.

NOTE 2.—For the transaction of business, 10 regents attending shall be a quorum; but the regents may elect an executive committee of not less than 7, which in the interval between the meetings may transact such business of the regents as they may authorize, except to grant or revoke charters, or grant honorary degrees.

Degrees and diplomas.—The regents may confer by diploma under their common seal such honorary degrees as they may deem proper, and may establish examinations as to attainments in learning, and award and confer suitable certificates, diplomas and degrees on persons who satisfactorily meet the requirements prescribed.

Examinations.—They shall establish in the academies of the university, examinations in studies furnishing a suitable standard of graduation from the academies and of admission to colleges, and certificates or diplomas shall be conferred on students who satisfactorily pass such examinations.

NOTE 1.—All the questions in arithmetic, geography, grammar, and spelling, up to June, 1882, are published with answers in a single volume called "The Regents Questions Complete, with Key", price $2.00. No other questions with answers have been published, but the questions alone for the preceding year may be had at any time in book form for 50 cts.

NOTE 2.—Any person shall be admitted to these academic examinations who shall conform to the rules and pay the fees prescribed by the regents, and said fees shall not exceed $1.00 for each academic branch and $5.00 for each higher branch in which the candidate is examined.

Control.—The university, including the State library and State museum, and such other departments as the regents may establish, is under the control of the regents, who have all the powers of trustees, including full authority to appoint all needed officers and employees; to fix their titles, duties, salaries and terms of service; to make all needed regulations to buy, sell, exchange or receive by will, gift or on deposit articles or collections properly pertaining thereto; to maintain lectures connected with higher education in this State; and to lend to or deposit permanently with other institutions books, specimens or other articles in their custody which, because of being duplicates or for other reasons, will, in the judgment of the regents, be more useful in the said institutions than if retained in the original collections at Albany.

State Publications.—The regents have charge of the preparation, publication, and distribution, whether by sale, exchange or gift, of the colonial history, natural history, and all other State publications not otherwise assigned by law.

To guard against the waste of destruction of State publications, and to provide for the completion of sets to be permanently preserved in American and foreign libraries, the regents maintain in the State library a duplicate department to which each State department, board, or bureau shall send not less than five copies of each of its publications when issued, and after completing its distribution, any remaining copies which it no longer requires. The above publications, with any other books and pamphlets not needed in the State library, constitute the duplicate department, and the rules for sale, exchange or distribution from it are fixed by the regents, who use all receipts from such exchanges or sales for the increase of the State library.

TABULAR ANALYSIS

INDEX

The Regents' Questions.

1. *The Regents' Questions* in Arithmetic, Geography, Grammar and Spelling from the first examination in 1866 to June 1882. (*No questions of later date will be printed.*) Being the 11,000 Questions for the preliminary examinations for admission to the University of the State of New York, prepared by the Regents of the University, and participated in simultaneously by more than 250 academies, forming a basis for the distribution of more than a million of dollars. *Complete with Key.* Cloth, 16mo, pp. 473. $2.00.

2. *Complete.* The same as above but without answers. Pp. 340. $1.00.

In the subjects named, no other Question Book can compare with this either in completeness, in excellence, or in popularity. By Legislative Enactment no lawyer can be admitted to the bar in the State of New York without passing a Regents' Examination in these subjects.

3. *Separately.* The same, each subject by itself, all Manilla, 16mo. *Arithmetic*, 1293 Questions, pp. 93, 25 cts. *Geography*, 1987 Questions, pp. 70, 25 cts. *Grammar*, 2976 Questions, pp. 109, 25 cts. *Spelling*, 4800 Words, pp. 61, 25 cts. *Keys to Arithmetic, Geography, and Grammar*, each 25 cts.

4. *The Dime Question Books*, with full answers, notes, queries, etc. Paper, pp. about 40. By A. P. SOUTHWICK. Each 10 cts.

Elementary Series.

3. Physiology.
4. Theory and Practice.
6. U. S. History and Civil Gov't.
10. Algebra.
13. American Literature.
14. Grammar.
15. Orthography and Etymology.
18. Arithmetic.
19. Physical and Political Geog.
20. Reading and Punctuation.

These 10 in one book. Cloth, $1.00.

Advanced Series.

1. Physics.
2. General Literature,
5. General History.
7. Astronomy.
8. Mythology.
9. Rhetoric.
11. Botany.
12. Zoölogy.
16. Chemistry.
17. Geology.

These 10 in one book. Cloth, $1.00.

Extra Volumes, 21. Temperance Physiology, 22. Book-Keeping, 23. Letter-Writing, each 10 cts.

The immense sale of the Regents' Questions in Arithmetic, Geography, Grammar, and Spelling has led to frequent inquiry for the questions in the Advanced Examinations. *As it is not permitted to reprint these*, we have had prepared this series, by which the teacher need purchase books only on the subjects upon which special help is needed. Frequently a $1.50 book is bought for the sake of a few questions in a single study. Here, the studies may be taken up one at a time, *a special advantage in New York, since applicants for State Certificates may now present themselves for examination in only part of the subjects, and receive partial Certificates to be exchanged for full Certificates when all the branches have been passed.* The same plan is very generally pursued by county superintendents and commissioners who are encouraging their teachers to prepare themselves for higher certificates.

5. *Quizzism. Quirks and Quibbles from Queer Quarters.* Being a Mélange of questions in Literature, Science, History, Biography, Mythology, Philology, Geography, etc. By A. P. SOUTHWICK. Cloth, 16mo, pp. 55. 25 cts. The same with Key, $1.00.

A stimulus for home study, and invaluable for school or teachers' gatherings.

6. *A Quiz-Book on the Theory and Practice of Teaching.* By A. P. SOUTHWICK. Cloth, 12mo, pp. 220. Price $1.00.

This is one of the six books recommended by the State Department for study in preparation for State Certificates.

C. W. BARDEEN, Publisher, Syracuse, N. Y.

Helps in Regents' Examinations.

1. *Regents' Examination Paper.* This is prepared from forms furnished by the Regents' office, and is of a weight and quality of paper chosen there as best fitted for the purpose. Each 1,000 half-sheets comes in a varnished wooden box with sliding cover, strong enough to bear shipment by express. The paper is printed in four forms, viz.: Whole sheets, Half-sheets, Spelling, and Book-Keeping in whole sheets. We suggest for most schools the following proportion:

Whole sheets, 350, equal to half-sheets	700
Half-sheets	100
Spelling	100
Book-Keeping, 50, equal to half-sheets	100
	1,000

We will however fill orders in any proportion desired, with the single proviso that all ordering must be in hundreds of half-sheets. We cannot undertake to count out, for instance, 737 whole sheets, 182 half-sheets, and 91 spelling. Orders will be received *only* for boxes holding the equivalent of 1,000 half-sheets, at the uniform rate of $3.00. As this is less than 25 cts. a pound, we can allow no discount whatever, even to the trade, and we prefer that all orders should come to us from the school direct.

NOTE. The demand for a paper that would answer all the requirements for the examination in drawing, led us to prepare a special paper of the size and quality approved by the Regents. This is uniform in size with the other paper, but is not included in the assortment put up in the boxes, because of the difference in weight and price. It costs $4.00 per ream, or $1.00 per 100 sheets, is of exceptional quality, and indispensable where the drawing examination is to be taken.

2. *Regents' Examination Pens.* These pens are put up in quarter-gross boxes, and will be sent post-paid for 25 cts. a quarter-gross or $1.00 a gross.

3. *Regents' Examination Record.* Principals who have tried it pronounce our New Record perfect. It contains an alphabetical index, a classified record of certificates and diplomas, and individual records for 432 pupils, with dates of all credits, pass-cards, certificates, and diplomas. Price $3.00. For large schools, a few have been bound up in canvass, double-size, for 834 pupils, price $6.00.

4. *Regents' Individual Card Records.* These give the same individual record as above, but are printed each separately on card-board. Price $1.50 a hundred.

5. *Syllabus of Regents' Examinations in American History.* These are published three months before each examination, and have been prepared from the beginning by Prof. Welland Hendrick of the Cortland State Normal school, author of "Brief History of the Empire State." The price is 50 cts. a dozen, and we advise principals to send in orders at least two months before the examination.

C. W. BARDEEN, Publisher, Syracuse, N. Y.

Locke (John). *Sketch of*, by R. H. Quick. Paper, 16mo, pp. 27. 15
Lowrie (R. W.) *How to obtain Greatest Benefit from a Book*. Paper, 8vo, pp. 12 25
McCully's *Perforated Erasers*, per doz 1 00
McKay (John S.) *100 Experiments in Natural Science*. Paper, 16mo, pp. 50 15
***Maps for the Wall.** Send for Special Circulars.

Maps **Relief Maps*. Switzerland, 11x17½, $3.50; 23x34, $10.00. Palestine.. 10 00
—*Dissected Maps* United States sawn into States 75
—*The same*, New York State sawn into Counties 75
—**Onondaga County*. Cloth, 4x4½ feet 10 00
Marble (A. P.) *Powers of School Officers*. Paper. 16mo, pp. 27......... 15
Marenholz-Buelow (Baroness) *School Work-shops*. Paper, 16mo, pp. 27. 15
—*Child and Child Nature*. Frœbel's Ed'l Theories. Cloth, 12mo, pp. 207.. 1 50
Maudsley (H.) *Sex in Mind and Education*. Paper, 16mo, pp. 42..... 15
Maxwell (W. H.) *Examinations as Tests for Promotion*. Paper, 8vo, pp. 11 15
—*The Text-Books of Comenius*, with cuts from the *Orbis Pictus*. 8vo, pp. 24 25
Meiklejohn (J. M. D.) *The New Education*. 16mo, pp. 35 15
—*An old Educational Reformer*. Dr. Andrew Bell. Cloth, 16mo, pp. 182... 1 00
Michael (O. S.) *Algebra for Beginners*. Cloth, 16mo, pp. 120................ 75
Mill (John Stuart.) *Inaugural Address at St. Andrews*. Paper, 8vo, pp. 31... 25
Miller (Warner.) *Education as a Dep't of Government*. Paper, 8vo, pp. 12. 15
Mills (C. D. B.) *The Tree of Mythology*. Cloth, 8vo, Pp. 281................ 3 00
Milne (James M.) *Teachers' Institutes, Past and Present*. Paper, 8vo, pp. 22.. 25
Milton (John) *A Small Tractate of Education*. Paper, 16mo, pp. 26...... 15
—*Sketch of*, by R. H. Quick. Paper, 16mo, pp 55 15
Minutes *of the International Congress of Education*, 1889. Cloth, 4 vols.... . 5 00
Missouri, *Civil Government of*, Northam. Cloth, 16mo, pp 151.............. 75
Monroe (Will S.) *Labors of Henry Barnard*. Leath , 16mo, pp. 35........ 50

New York *Question Book*, with all the Questions of the Uniform, State, Cornell, Scholarship, and Normal Entrance Examinations, to March 31, 1890, *with Answers*. Cloth, 8vo, pp. 461.. 1 00
—*The same*, Supplement No. 1, to June, 1891. Paper, 8vo, pp. 63.. 25
—*The same*, Supplement No. 2, to June, 1892. Paper, 8vo, pp. 139.... 25
—*The same*, Questions in Drawing to Date. Paper, 16mo. 25
—*The same*, Questions in School Law and Civil Gov't. Paper, 16mo....... 25
—*State Examination Questions* to date. Cloth, 16mo, pp. 402..... .... 1 00
—*The Questions in Book-Keeping, with Answers*. Paper, 16mo, pp. 31..... 10
—*History of the Empire State*, Hendrick. Cloth, 12mo, pp. 203 75
—*Civil Government of the State of*, Northam. Cloth, 16mo, pp. 185.......... 75
—*Code of Public Instruction*. Latest Edition 2 50
—*Natural History*, and *Cabinet Reports*. Write for information.

Northam (Henry C.) *Civil Government*. Cloth, 16mo, pp. 231.......... 75
—*The same for Missouri*. Cloth, 16mo, pp. 151................................ 75
—*Fixing the Facts of American History*. Cloth, 16mo, pp. 300.............. 75
—*Conversational Lessons Leading to Geography*. Paper, 16mo, pp. 39...... 25
Northend (Chas.) *Memory Selections*. Three series. Each.............. 25
Northrop (B. G.) *High Schools*. Paper, 8vo, pp. 26........................ 25
Northrup (A. J.) *Camps and Tramps in the Adirondacks*. 16mo, pp. 302. 1 25
Number Lessons. On card-board, 7x11, after the Grube Method.......... 10
Page (David P.) *The Theory and Practice of Teaching*. 16mo, pp. 448. Manilla, 50 cts.; Cloth.. 1 00
Pardon (Emma L.) *Oral Instruction in Geography*. Paper, 16mo, pp. 29.... 15
Parsons (James Russell, Jr.,) *Prussian Schools through American Eyes*. Cloth, 8vo, pp. 91 .... 1 00
—*French Schools through American Eyes*. Cloth, 8vo, pp. 130...........1 00
Payne (Joseph.) *Lectures on the Art of Education*. Cloth, 16mo, pp. 281.. 1 00
Payne (W. H.) *A Short History of Education*. Cloth, 16mo, pp. 105.... 50
Pedagogical Primers. Manilla, 16mo, pp. 40, each 25
1. School Management, pp. 45. 2. Letter-Writing, pp. 37.

Perez (B.) *The First Three Years of Childhood*. Cloth, 16mo, pp. 295....... 1 50
—*Tiedemann's Record of Infant Life*. Manilla, pp. 46.................. ... 15

Periodicals. *The School Bulletin*. Monthly, 16 pp., 10x14. Per year...... 1 00
— Bound Vols. I-XIX. Cloth, 200 pp., each...................................... 2 00
—*The School Room*. Bound volumes I-V. Each 1 50
—*The New Education*. Vol. VI 2 00

Pestalozzi (J. H.) *His Aim and Work*, by De Guimps. 12mo, pp. 296...... 1 50
—*Sketch of*, by R. H. Quick. Paper, 16mo, pp. 40....... 15
—*Pestalozzian Arithmetics*, by J. H. Hoose. Boards, 16mo, 1st Year, pp. 217. 2d Year, pp. 236. Each.. 50

——*Lessons on Number and Form*, by C. Reiner. Cloth, 16mo, pp. 439...... 3 00
Pick (Dr. E.) *Dr. Pick's French Method.* Leatherette, 16mo, pp. 118...... 1 00
——*Memory, and the Rational Means of Improving it.* Cloth, 16mo, pp. 193... 1 00
Pitcher (James.) *Outlines of Surveying and Navigation.* Cloth, 16mo, pp. 121 50
Plumb (Chas. G.) *Map Drawing of New York.* Manilla, 8vo, pp. 16........ 25
Pooler (Chas. T.) *Chart of Civil Government.* Sheets 12x18, per hundred.. 5 00
——*Hints on Teaching Orthoepy.* Paper, 16mo, pp. 15........................ 10
Preece (Mrs. Louise.) *Physical Culture and Voice Work.* Leath., 16mo, pp. 102 75
——*The Same, Analyzed and Illustrated.* Cloth, 4to, pp. 292.................. 2 00
Prentice (Mrs. J. B.) *Review Problems in Arithmetic.* Paper, 16mo, pp. 93. 20
——*Key to the above.* Paper, 16mo, pp. 20 25
——*Review Questions in Geography.* Paper, 16mo, pp. 48..................... 15
Primer *of School Management.* Manilla, pp. 45............................ 25
——*of Letter-Writing.* Manilla, pp. 37...................................... 25
Quick (R. H.) *Essays on Educational Reformers.* Cloth, 12mo, pp., 331 .... 1 55
Redway (J. W.) *School Geography of Pennsylvania.* Leather'te, 16mo, pp. 98 35
***Regents' Examination Paper.** Per 1000 half-sheets in box.............. 3 00
Regents' Examination Pens. ¼ Gross, 25c. Per Gross, post-paid...... 1 00
Regents' Fourth Year Latin. *Cæsar's Conspiracy.* Paper, 16mo, pp. 20 10
Regents' Selections *in American, German, and French Literature.* Leatherette, pp. 56. 25 cents. Each separate, paper.......................... 10
Regents' Examination Record. For 432 scholars, $3.00; 864 scholars.. 6 00
Regents' Examination Syllabus, in U. S. History. Paper, per dozen,.. 50
Regents' Questions. *To June, 1882. (No later are printed). Eleven Editions.*

1. *Complete with Key.* Cloth, 16mo, pp. 476.............................. 2 00
2. *Complete.* The same as the above, but without the answers. Pp. 333. 1 00
3. *Arithmetic.* The 1,293 questions in Arithmetic. Pp. 93.......... 25
4. *Key to Arithmetic*, Answers to the above. Manilla, 16mo, pp. 20.... 25
6. *Geography*, The 1,987 questions in Geography. Pp. 70......... 25
7. *Key to Geography.* Answers to the above. Manilla, 16mo, pp. 36.... 25
8. *Grammar.* The 2,976 questions in Grammar. Manilla, 16mo, pp. 109 25
9. *Grammar and Key.* Cloth, 16mo, pp. 198........................ 1 00
10. *Key to Grammar.* Manilla, 16mo, pp. 88........................ 25
11. *Spelling.* The 4,800 words given in Spelling. Manilla, 16mo, pp. 61. 25

Rein (W.) *Outlines of Pedagogics.* Cloth, 12mo, pp. 208.................... 1 25
Richardson (B. W.) *Learning and Health.* Paper, 16mo, pp. 39.......... 15
Robinson (A. H.) *Numeral School Register.* Manilla, folio, pp. 16........... 25
Rousseau (J. J.) *Sketch of*, by R. H. Quick. Paper, 16mo, pp. 30.......... 15
Rooper (T. G.) "*A Pot of Green Feathers.*" Leatherette, 16mo, pp. 591.. 50
——*Object Teaching or Words and Things.* Leatherette, 16mo, pp. 56 50
Ryan (G. W.) *School Record.* 56 blanks on each of 14 sheets............. 50
Sabin (Henry) "*Organization*" *vs. Individuality.* Paper, 8vo, pp. 9 25
Sanford (H. R.) *The Word Method in Number.* Per box of 45 cards. 50
——*The Limited Speller.* Leatherette, 16mo, pp. 104 35
Schepmoes (A. E.) *Rise of the New York School System.* Leath., 16mo, pp. 32 35
School Room Classics. 11 vols. Paper, 16mo, pp. about 40, each........ 15

I. Huntington's *Unconscious Tuition.*
II. Fitch's *Art of Questioning.*
III. Kennedy's *Philosophy of School Discipline.*
IV. Fitch's *Art of Securing Attention.*
V. Richardson's *Learning and Health.*
VI. Meiklejohn's *New Education.*
VII. Milton's *Tractate of Education.*
VIII. Von Buelow's *School Workshop.*
IX. Maudsley's *Sex in Mind and in Education.*
X. *Education as Viewed by Thinkers.*
XI. Harris's *How to Teach Natural Science in the Public Schools.*
XII. Dickinson's *Oral Teaching.*
XIII. Tiedemann's *Record of Infant Life*
XIV. Butler's *Place of Comenius in Education.*
XV. Harris's *Theory of Education.*

Schreber (D. G. R.) *Home Exercise for Health and Cure.* Cloth, 16mo, pp. 91 50
Shaw's *Scholar's Register*, Paper, 5x7, pp. 16. Per dozen....... 50
Sheely (Aaron) *Anecdotes and Humors of School Life.* Cloth, 12mo, pp. 350 1 50
Sherrill (J. E.) *The Normal Question Book.* Cloth. 12mo, pp. 405........ 1 50
Shirreff (Emily). *The Kindergarten System.* Cloth, 12mo, pp. 200.......... 1 00
Skinner (Chas. R.) *The Arbor Day Manual.* Cloth, 8vo, pp. 475.............. 2 50
——*The New York Question Book.* Cloth, 8vo, pp. 461 .... 2 00
Smith (C. F.) *Honorary Degrees in American Colleges.* Paper, 8vo, pp. 9... 15
Smith (Edward.) *History of the Schools of Syracuse.* Cloth, 8vo, pp. 347....... 3 00
Smith (Geo. M.) *Vocabulary to Cæsar's Gallic War.* Cloth, 16mo, pp. 67.. 50
Smith (Wm.) *Geometry Test Papers.* Package of 100, 8½x10................ 1 00
Song Budget, *The.* 186th *Thousand.* Paper, small 4to pp. 76, ... 15
Song Century, *The.* Paper, small 4to, pp. 87.............................. 15

Song Patriot, *The.* Paper, small 4to, pp. 80 15
Song Budget Music Series, including all the above. Cloth, pp. 243.... 50
Songs from Arbor Day Manual. Manilla, 8vo, pp. 60........ 25
Songs of the Lyceum League. Leatherette, 4to, pp. 48........ 20
Sornberger (S. J.) *Normal Language Lessons,* Boards, 16mo, pp. 75..... 50
Southwick (A. P.) *Twenty Dime Question Books,* with full answers, notes, queries, etc. Paper, 16mo, pp. about 40. Each........ 10

Elementary Series.	Advanced Series.
3. Physiology.	1. Physics.
4. Theory and Practice.	2. General Literature.
6. U. S. History and Civil Gov't.	5. General History.
10. Algebra.	7. Astronomy.
13. American Literature.	8. Mythology.
14. Grammar	9. Rhetoric.
15. Orthography and Etymology	11. Botany.
18. Arithmetic.	12. Zoology.
19. Physical and Political Geog.	16. Chemistry.
20. Reading and Punctuation.	17. Geology.
The 10 in one book, cloth, $1.00.	The 10 in one book, cloth, $1.00.

——*Extra Numbers,* edited by C. W. Bardeen, 21. Temperance Physiology; 22. Book-Keeping; 23. Letter-Writing. Each........ 10
——*Quizzism.* Quirks and Quibbles from Queer Quarters. 16mo, pp. 25.... 25
——*A Quiz Book of Theory and Practice.* Cloth, 12mo, pp. 220........ 1 00
Spencer (Herbert). *Education, Intellectual, Moral, and Physical.* 16mo, pp. 300. Manilla, 50 cts.; Cloth........ 1 00
Standard Teachers' Library. Includes Laurie's *Comenius,* Carlisle's *Memoirs,* Page's *Theory and Practice,* DeGuimp's *Pestalozzi,* Spencer's *Education,* DeGraff's *Guide,* Tate's *Philosophy,* etc. Each, paper. 50
Steven, (Wm.) *History of the Edinburgh High School.* Cloth, 16mo, pp. 590 2 00
Stilwell (Lamont) *Practical Question Book.* Cloth, 12mo, pp. 400........ 1 50
Stowell (T. B.) *Syllabus of Lectures on Physiology.* Boards, 8vo, pp. 133.. 1 00
Straight (H. H.) *Aspects of Industrial Education.* Paper, 8vo, pp. 12..... 15
Swett (John) *Manual of Elocution.* Cloth, 12mo, pp. 300, *net*........ 1 50
Tate (Thos.) *The Philosophy of Education.* Cloth, 16mo, pp. 330....... 1 50
Taylor (H. F.) *Union School Record Cards* 5x8 inches. Per hundred.......2 00
Thomas (Flavel S.) *University Degrees.* Paper, 16mo, pp. 40........ 15
Thousand Questions *in U. S. History.* Cloth, 16mo, pp. 200........ 1 00
Thoughts *from Earnest Women.* Paper, 16mo, pp. 36........ 15
Tiedemann (D.) *Record of Infant Life.* Paper, 16mo, pp. 46........ 15
Tillinghast (Wm.) *The Diadem of School Songs.* Boards, 4to, pp. 160. ... 50
Underwood (L. M.) *Systematic Plant Record.* Manilla, 7x8¼ pp. 52...... 30
Uniform Examination Paper, for Commissioners. 500 sheets........ 3 00
Uniform Examination Questions, *New York,* to March 1889.

I. Arithmetic,	317	Questions, 10 cents.	II.	Key, 10 cents.
III. Geography,	709	" "	IV.	" "
V. Grammar,	533	" "	VI.	" "
VII. U. S. History,	429	" "	VIII.	" "
IX. Civil Government	354	" "	X.	" "
XI. Physiology,	345	" "	XII.	" "

☞ *See also* NEW YORK.
Van Wie (C. B.) *Outlines in U. S. History.* Paper, 16mo, pp. 40 and map 15
——*Development Helps.* Leatherette, 16mo, pp. 100........ 50
——*Methods in Common Branches.* Cloth, 16mo, pp. 197........ 75
Welch (Emma A.) *Intermediate Arithmetic Problems.* Cloth, 16mo, pp. 172 75
——*Key* to the above, Cloth, 16mo, pp. 30........ 50
Wells (C. R.) *Natural Movement Series of Writing Books.* Nos. 1, 2, per dozen 84 cts. Nos. 3-5........ 96
——*Manual of the Movement Method in Writing.* Paper, 4to, pp. 44. *Ill.*....... 25
——*A Lesson on Arm Movement in Writing.* Paper, 8vo, pp. 32........ 25
Wheatley (Wm. A.) *German Declensions Simplified.* Paper, 16mo, pp. 53... 25
Wilkin (Eva) *Map Drawing Book of the Continents.* Boards, 4to, pp. 48, 75
——*Map Drawing Book of the United States.* Boards, pp. 37........ 75
——*Descriptive Geography taught by means of Map Drawing.* Teachers' Edition. Boards, 4to, pp. 129, with 49 Maps........ 1 50
Williams (Geo. A.) *Topics in American History.* Cloth, 16mo, pp. 50.... 50
Williams (S. G.) *History of Modern Education.* Cloth, 16mo, pp. 395 .... 1 50
Wilson (J. D.) *English Grammar Made Practical.* Cloth, 16mo, pp. 112. 75
——*Elementary English.* Leatherette, 16mo, pp. 67........ 35
Yawger (Rose N.) *How to celebrate Arbor Day.* Paper, 16mo, pp. 14 15
——*The Indian and the Pioneer.* Cloth, 8vo, pp. 335..$3.00 or Two Volumes.... 3 50

www.ingramcontent.com/pod-product-compliance
Lightning Source LLC
Chambersburg PA
CBHW032357280326
41935CB00008B/613

* 9 7 8 3 3 3 7 3 7 3 5 9 7 *